COOKIN' with COCKY

MORE THAN A COOKBOOK

Charlie & Alex Hawkins

LONGSTREET
Athens, Georgia

Published by
Longstreet Press
325 Milledge Avenue
Athens, Georgia 30601

Printed in The United States of America

1st printing, 2004

ISBN: 1-56352-742-1

Book and jacket design by Burtch Hunter Design LLC

Our thanks to Tom Price, Emily White, Kerry Tharp, Myrna and Loran Smith
and Eddie Elmore for their help in putting this book together,
and our special thanks to you loyal Gamecock fans
for sharing your recipes and pictures
with Charlie and myself.

Dedication

This cookbook is dedicated to the greatest and most loyal football fans in the country. That would be, of course, the University of South Carolina Gamecock fans. Those 80,000 plus fans that turn out every fall win or lose, to cheer for their Cocks. That same 80,000 plus fans who will fill the stands again this fall.

How can you make such a statement, some will ask? How about the 84,000 fans at Alabama? The 86,000 at Auburn, the 92,000 at Georgia, another 88,000 at Florida and 104,000 screaming fans at Tennessee. Did you forget about them?

Let me answer that by asking one simple question. Isn't it more fun to win than to lose? In the 110 year history of Gamecock football we have lost more games than we have won. 509 loses & 499 wins. Our longest winning streak was 7 consecutive seasons and that was from 1928-1934, which is a long time ago. Win or lose, our fans kept coming. Admittedly they sometimes leave a little early, but they are always back the next game, or the next season with renewed optimism and hope. The same as it will be in 2004.

It's easy to understand how these other teams draw these large crowds. Everybody loves a winner. Over the past twenty years Georgia and Alabama have endured only four losing seasons. Auburn has had but three. Tennessee has had only one and Florida hasn't had a deficit season since 1979.

Meanwhile, the Gamecocks over that same period of time had 11 losing seasons and only 9 winning ones.

Despite these dismal facts the Carolina fans keep showing up in ever growing numbers. In the last six years over 80,000 plus fans rank 9th in Division A college attendance. After losing 21 straight games in 1998 1999, we averaged 82,000 fans at our home games in the year 2000. Now our stadium only seats 80,250, so how can you sell more seats than you've got? Simply by having the best fans of any team in college football.

The various "Bowls" love us because we bring 35,000 of these loyalist with us when we come.

So when September 11th rolls around and the Georgia Bulldogs come to town, look for another oversold house at Williams Brice Stadium. You fans are without question the greatest. I rest my case.

Tailgating

No one seems to know when tailgating first started. I imagine they were doing some form of it in the early 1890's. So I posed the question to Dom Fusci, the oldest living Gamecock player. He replied, "How in the hell would I know, I was playing not tailgating. But I guess they were, he added, cause everyone was drunk by the time the game was over."

I know that tailgating has been a big part of college football for many years, but twenty years ago Gamecock fans took it to a new dimension.

When that man in black, Joe Morrison, won the first nine games in 1984 and went on to finish with a 10-2 season the Gamecock fans went totally berserk. I've never seen anything like it. The excitement was electrifying. How about those Cocks? I've got to go buy something black. I've got to buy anything black.

In anticipation of the coming season, businessman Ed Robinson bought some property on the south side of the stadium, paved it, fenced it in and built a clubhouse with electricity, running water, sewer connection, cable television, heating and air conditioning. He named it CAROLINA PARK and offered for sale 89, 9x16 parking spaces with permanent ownership for $7,500 each. He and Doc Howard got on the phone and sold out in less than four hours. Luxury tailgating was off and running.

The following year (1987) Ken Wheat, working for and with Boyd Management followed suit with COCKS CORNER. They had room for 170 parking spaces that sold out in three days at an average price of $7,500.

Even though Joe Morrison's Black magic had suddenly turned south, winning only three games, luxury parking was headed up, up, up. There was no stopping it.

The next year (1987) three businessmen followed suit with STADIUM PLACE. The price had gone up to $9,950, and the number of spaces had increased to 240. They sold all they wanted, keeping some places set aside for leasing.

Joe Lee Dunn's Fire Ants defense was back on top with an 8-4 record and the optimism and excitement was too. Just wait until next year, or the following year, who cares, tailgating is so damn much fun and we do love our Cocks.

In 1990 Ed Robinson bought the unused railroad tracks at the south end of the stadium. He obtained 22 railroad cabooses. Put them on the tracks, painted them Garnet and Black and sold them for $45,000 a piece. It surprised no one that they sold all 22 cabooses in a matter of days. The average total investment for the "COCK A BOOSE RAILROAD" is $100,000. It didn't hurt that Joe Morrison's Gamecocks went to another bowl, but by now Carolina tailgaters wished that all bowls be played at Williams Brice Stadium.

In 1995, Ed Bignon acquired some land within field goal distance of the stadium and developed UNIVERSITY HOUSE. He had no trouble selling all of its 168 parking spaces at $12,000 a pop.

The same year John Quenneville found some land on Key Road within punting distance on the east side of the stadium and quickly sold another 127 spaces and called it THE TOUCHDOWN ZONE.

When Lou Holtz went 8-4 in 2000 and 9-3 in 2001, with back to back bowl victories the hysteria soon followed. That got the attention of former Gamecock quarterback Terry Bishop and former Georgia quarterback and coach Ray Goff. They took over what had been PIGSKIN PARK. They made some necessary changes, including a $400,000 clubhouse and renamed it "THE COOP". This added another 300 parking spaces which they sold for $10,500.

Back came John Quennesville with TOUCHDOWN ZONE 11 with another 163 spaces, plus 15 cabooses. Along with the purchase of a caboose you also get 5 parking spaces for only $200,000. To date they have only one caboose left and all of this was in the wake of back-to-back 5-7 seasons.

In other words, Carolina tailgaters have 1,267 private parking spaces, six clubhouses, 37 cabooses, to our opponents-zero.

No other school has these facilities for their tailgating followers. So while we may not always win on the scoreboard, nobody can beat us at partying.

Introduction

The most obvious question that comes to mind is why would Alex Hawkins, a native West Virginian, think he could write a cookbook?

No one ever suggested that West Virginia is the culinary capitol of the universe. I grew up on meat and potatoes, salt and pepper. Cook it fast and burn it. I didn't even like my mother's cooking and I'd never tasted anyone else's.

Then I met Charlie and my appreciation for food escalated. Charlie is my wife of five years, but I have known her for over twenty years. There are a number of things that Charlie can't do, but cooking is not one of them. Charlie is without a doubt the finest cook I have ever known. I am not alone in my thinking. But, it didn't come easily or quickly.

She grew up in Butler, Georgia in a family of relative affluence. She had three maids that worked six and a half days a week. Neither she, nor her mother ever cooked a meal.

It was in Atlanta when her husband Henry, and his two friends, brought some freshly caught fish home and asked Charlie to fry them. He entertained while Charlie went into the kitchen and called Katie, the family maid, in Butler, to find out how to fry fish.

Katie said, Baby just put some salt in some meal and roll the fish in it. Put some lard in an iron skillet and get it real hot then drop the fish in. Brown it crisp and drain it on a paper sack. Charlie did exactly what Katie had told her.

At the dinner table, minutes later, they took their first bite and looked at each other and then at Charlie. Did you scale the fish, asked Henry? Scale, she nodded negatively. Did you gut them, Henry inquired? Gut them, she responded? She of course had done neither. They finished dinner at The Chateaubriand Restaurant.

The next day, out of embarrassment or whatever, Charlie drove home to Butler and spent the next three weeks, going from house to house, in Butler and neighboring towns learning all she could from the best cooks available. She was 22 years old when she cooked her first meal.

Some eight states, two countries, 600 cookbooks and 40 years later, Charlie has developed some terrific recipes that I know you will enjoy. No, I'm not worried about writing a cookbook. In fact I am a little **COCKY**.

COOKIN' with COCKY

2004 Schedule

September 4	at **Vanderbilt***
September 11	**Georgia***
September 18	**South Florida**
September 25	**Troy State**
October 2	at **Alabama***
October 9	**Ole Miss***
October 16	at **Kentucky***
October 30	**Tennessee***
November 6	**Arkansas***
November 13	at **Florida***
November 20	at **Clemson**

*SEC Game

APPETIZERS

Marinated Vegetable Snack ~ **Billy Canada**

Asparagus Roll-ups ~ **Diane & Steve Lipscomb**

Pickled Shrimp ~ **Kay & Eddie Floyd**

Cheese-Olive Snack ~ **Susie & Heyward King**

Marinated Shrimp ~ **Zoe & Alex Sanders**

Gamecock Oyster and Shrimp Bowl ~ **Caroline & Don Bailey**

Carolina Ham & Cheese Rolls ~ **Augusta & King Dixon**

Jalapeno-Tomatillo Salsa ~ **Sherrill R. Bland**

Chicken Crispy Bites w/ Peach Snapps ~ **Frederick M. Zeigler**

Marinated Cheese ~ **Dick Harris**

Mushrooms stuffed ~ **Cathy & Gerald Sease**

Deviled Eggs ~ **Chery & Ken Wheat**

Swedish Pickled Shrimp ~ **Mozella & Harold White**

Parmesan Chicken Wings ~ **Elizabeth & Bill Jerry**

Hot'n Nutty ~ **Diane & Steve Lipscomb**

Shrimp Pate ~ **Kathi & Jimmy Mitchell**

Deviled Eggs ~ **Betty & Don Barton**

Mexican Pie ~ **Becky & Lem Harper**

Ham Roll Ups ~ **Lynne McCartha**

Marinated Shrimp ~ **Susie & Heyward King**

Sausage Roll Ups ~ **Dona Fowler**

Sugar and Spice Pecans ~ **Annali & Red Furguson**

Basil Spread ~ **Mary Ella Wright**

Blackeye Pea Cocktail Balls ~ **Frances Fulmer**

Cheddar & Bacon Log ~ **Curtis Frye**

Cheese & Beef Roll-ups ~ **Jimmy Knight**

Jalopeno Roll-ups ~ **Tommy Addison**

Party Nibbler ~ **Johnny Gregory**

Spinich Balls ~ **Frances Fulmer**

Pickled Shrimp ~ **Rachel & Governor Jim Hodges**

Cream Cheese Salsa ~ **Janice Marthers**

Lobster Pate' ~ **Kathi & Jim Mitchell**

Scott's "Hot and Spicy" BBQ chicken wings ~ **Jean & Jim Poole**

Nacho Mama's Salsa ~ **Howard Hughes**

Deviled Eggs ~ **Alice Flansburg**

Tortilla Roll-ups ~ **Howard Hughes**

Deviled Eggs ~ **Trish Norris**

BILLY CANADA

There are only a few things in life that don't change. Billy Canada is one of those things. While his wives do vary from time to time and his waste line has expanded he is basically the same "Nose" that I knew when we were fraternity brothers in the late fifties.

He is never boring or unexciting to be around because Nose, manufactures his own fun. He was one of the first members of Carolina Park. He was on the board of directors and is their self appointed spokesman.

When asked to submit one recipe, he offered up twenty. "I speak for my people", he calmly explained.

His Car Bar is legendary as is his growing of tomatoes. "There ain't nothing to cookin," says Nose. "All you've got to be in smarter than the stove."

Trust him not when you are gambling.

Marinated Vegetable Snack
BILLY (NOSE) CANADA

2 carrots, cut into sticks
1 cup broccoli buds
1 cup cauliflowerets
1 medium cucumber, sliced
1 medium zucchini, cut into sticks
1 small onion, sliced and separated into rings
½ cup cooking oil
3 tablespoons white wine vinegar
1 teaspoon dried oregano, crushed
½ teaspoon salt
¼ teaspoon pepper

Advanced preparation: In saucepan simmer carrots, covered, in small amount of water for 2 minutes. Add broccoli and cauliflower; bring to boililng. Reduce heat; simmer 3 minutes more. Drain. Combine all vegetables. Combine cooking oil, vinegar, oregano, salt and pepper; pour over vegetables. Cover. Chill at least 8 hours; stir occasionally. Servings: 4 cups.

Asparagus Roll-Ups
DIANA & STEVE LIPSCOMB

16 thin slices ham
16 thin slices American white cheese
1 pack Lipton onion soup
8 oz. Sour cream

Steam asparagus and marinate in lemon juice. Mix Lipton Onion soup and sour cream. Layer mixture on ham slices, cheese, and asparagus. Spread thin. Roll ham lengthwise and refrigerate. Easy and good. Enjoy

Pickled Shrimp

KAY BAKER FLOYD

4½ - 5 lbs. cooked peeled shrimp, chilled
3 small lemons sliced thin
2-3 small onions sliced thin
3-4 jars button mushrooms drained
3-4 jars hearts of artichokes drained and quartered
Jar of capers drained
2-3 jars Italian dressing drain off oil
½ c salad vinegar with 1 tablespoon of horseradish
Celery seed

Mix and chill. Keep two weeks

Cheese-Olive Cocktail Snack

SUSIE & HEYWARD KING

1 cup medium cheddar cheese, grated
¼ cup butter

½ cup plain flour
¼ teaspoon red pepper, ground
Salt to taste
25 medium stuffed green olives

Combine all ingredients, except olives; mix until smooth and creamy. Mold mixture around each olive. Bake 10-12 minutes at 400 degrees. 25 servings.

Marinated Shrimp

ZOE & ALEX SANDERS
FROM HER BOOK *ENTERTAINING AT COLLEGE OF CHARLESTON*

1½ quarts. water
1½ teaspoons salt
1 bay leaf
2½ pounds medium shrimp, unpeeled
½ pound medium-size fresh mushrooms, washed and quartered
1 (14 oz.) can artichoke hearts, drained and quartered
1 (2oz.) jar capers, drained
1 jumbo yellow onion, thinly sliced
2 lemons, thinly sliced
3-gallon pot
3-gallon glass or plastic container with lid

MARINADE

1½ package Good Seasons Italian Dressing mix
½ cup vegetable oil
6 tablespoons apple cider vinegar
4 tablespoons water
1½ teaspoons prepared creamed horseradish

TO BOIL SHRIMP: *Use fast method for boiling shrimp*

TO MAKE MARINADE: *Whisk together Italian Dressing mix, oil, vinegar, water and horseradish.*

TO ASSEMBLE: *Layer mushrooms, artichoke hearts, capers, onions, and lemons in 3-gallon container and pour marinade over all. Refrigerate over night, turning container upside down and shaking it at least 4 times.*

An hour before serving, add shrimp and toss several times. When ready to serve, drain and arrange in glass bowl or platter for used skewers near shrimp.

Gamecock Oyster and Shrimp Bowl
CAROLINE & DON BAILEY

1 qt. Oyster
5 lb. Shrimp
Budweiser Beer
Saltines
Boiled peanuts

Boil shrimp until just pink. Add oysters. Drink Budweiser, Put shrimp and oysters in bowl with a bed of lettuce. Serve with saltines and boiled peanuts and more Budweiser.

KING DIXON

While at Carolina, King was an honor student, Phi Beta Kappa. He was Vice President of the freshman, sophomore and junior classes. He graduated Cumlaude in 1959.

After college he spent 22 years in the marines where he won a Bronze and Silver Star.

After service King returned to Laurens and was vice president of the local bank.

In 1987 King was named Athletic Director and served in that capacity for 6 years. He then returned to his bank job in Laurens.

King is, of course, a member of the school and state Hall of Fame. He has never been divorced, had a DUI and he has never spent the night in jail.

CONTINUED

But what does all that have to say about somebody? Nothing!

In 1957 we were playing a night game against the University of Texas, down in Austin. King had an upset stomach and wasn't sure he could play. He, never the less, fielded the opening kickoff on the two yard line and raced down the right side line, untouched for 80 yards when on or about the 20 yard line he soiled himself... That's right he messed in his white pants before 50,000 or so people. All of them good God Faring Texans. I was never so embarrassed in my life.

But King, well, he just crossed the goal line, dropped the ball in the end zone and kept right on running to the dressing room like nothing had happened.

It mattered not that we went on to beat the Longhorns; the damage had already been done.

It was the first and last time that we ever played the U.T. We were never invited back and all because of one King Dixon.

Carolina Ham and Cheese Delights

AUGUSTA & KING DIXON

2 packages small rolls
¾ lb. ham slices
1 stick margarine, melted
3 heaping tablespoons mustard
1 teaspoon Worcestershire
1 small onion, grated
1 teaspoon poppy seed

Mix together margarine, mustard, Worcestershire, onion, and poppy seed.

Slice rolls in half lengthwise. With pastry brush spread mixture on both sides. Put layer of ham slices, topped with grated cheese. Put rolls together. Bake at

350 degrees for 10-12 minutes or until cheese melts. Do Not Cover While Baking. These freeze well.

Jalapen-Tomatillo Salsa

SHERRILL BLAND

8-12 tomatillos, parboiled, after removing husks
4-6 New Mexico chiles, parboiled, after removing seeds and pith
1 small onion, chopped
2 garlic cloves, minced
1 teaspoon lime juice or vinegar
1-2 jalapeños, chopped
¼ cup fresh cilantro, chopped

After peeling and discarding the husks, drop the

tomatillos in boiling water for 4 minutes or until they soften slightly. Do the same with the chiles and the jalapenos. Let them each cool. Puree the tomatillos in the blender, then add, one after another, chiles, jalapeños, onion and garlic. Add lime juice or vinegar to taste. Complete the salsa by blending in the cilantro.

Chicken Crispy Bites with Peach Snapps-Apricot Sauce

FREDERICK M. ZEIGLER

1 lb. (or more) boneless chicken cut into bite size pieces (or shrimp)

MIXTURE
2 cloves garlic, minced
1 tablespoon ginger, minced
1 tablespoon lemon juice
1 tablespoon soy sauce
¾ cup almonds, finely ground
¼ cup sesame seeds
2 cups olive oil, extra virgin

SAUCE
2 tablespoons peach schnapps
½ cup apricot preserves
1 teaspoon dry mustard
1 teaspoon boiling water
1 tablespoon lemon juice

Marinade chicken over night in mixture. Drop chicken pieces into hot oil and cook until golden brown. (cooking time approximately 15 minutes).
Prepare sauce night before if you prefer chilled, or day of, if you prefer room temperature.
Serve to tailgaters, and enjoy.

Marinated Cheese with Peppers and Olives

DICK HARRIS
COURTESY OF LAND 'O LAKES

Marinate cheese cubes, red peppers and ripe olives for an easy make-ahead appetizer.

¼ cup olive or vegetable oil
12 oz. (about 2 cups) Land 'O Lakes chedarella, or cheddar cheese, cut into ¾ inch cubes
2 red bell peppers cut into ¾ inch pieces
1 (14 oz. can whole pitted ripe olives, drained
1 tablespoon white vinegar
½ teaspoon dried basil leaves
½ teaspoon dried oregano leaves
½ teaspoon finely chopped fresh garlic

Stir together all ingredients in medium bowl. Cover; refrigerate at least 4 hours or overnight. Serves 6.

Mushrooms, Stuffed

CATHY & GERALD SEASE

25 to 30 mushrooms, cleaned and stemmed
1 pound pork sausage
1 teaspoon Worcestershire sauce
1 teaspoon chopped garlic
½ teaspoon ground sage
½ pound shredded cheddar cheese
Shredded mozzarella cheese

After mushrooms have been cleaned and stemmed —

CONTINUED

reserve several stems and chop finely; set aside. Place mushroom caps in 1-inch deep boiler pan, cap side down.

In fry pan, brown and crumble sausage; add Worcestershire sauce, chopped garlic, chopped mushroom stems, and sage. When completely cooked, add cheddar cheese and stir until well blended. Maintain on low heat to keep sausage/cheese mixture pliable.

Fill each mushroom cap with approx. 1 teaspoon of pork/cheese mixture—depending upon size of cap. Use all mixture. Sprinkle finished caps with mozzarella cheese. Bake at 350 degrees for approx. 10-12 minutes.

Good idea to line broiler pan with tin foil to hold water cooked from mushrooms.

Serve: For tailgating, line Tupperware with tin foil and paper towels to absorb any extra moisture. Close tightly. Will stay warm until we get there. Okay even when cooled because there's no grease or water from mushrooms.

Deviled Eggs
CHERYL & KEN WHEAT

1 Dozen eggs
Mayonnaise, to taste
Sweet pickle relish, to taste
Salt and pepper, to taste
Paprika, Dash

Boil eggs, run under cold water as you peel the eggs to cool. Slice the eggs in half and scoop the yellow into a bowl. Mash with fork. Add mayonnaise, sweet pickle relish, salt and pepper. Mix all ingredients well and put by spoonfuls into egg halves.

Sprinkle with paprika and keep cold

Swedish Pickled Shrimp
MOZELLA & HAROLD WHITE

MARINADE
1½ cups salad oil
¾ cups white vinegar
3 tablespoons capers and juice
1 teaspoon celery seed
1½ teaspoon salt
Few drops of Tabasco

Combine all above ingredients. Mix well and set aside.

2½ lbs. frozen shrimp
¼ cup mixed pickling spices
1 tablespoon salt
2 cups sliced onions (optional)
7-8 bay leaves

Cover shrimp with boiling water. Add pickling spices and salt. Cover and simmer 5 minutes. Drain and cool with cold water. Alternate shrimp, onion and bay leaves in shallow dish. Pour marinade over shrimp. Cover. Chill at least 24 hours before serving.

Will keep a week in the refrigerator.

One of our favorites for parties. From: cooks.com.

Hot 'n Nutty

DIANE & STEVE LIPSCOMB

2 cups sharp cheddar cheese, grated
2 cups pecans, chopped
4–5 spring onions, chopped
2 tablespoons mayonnaise

Mix all the above ingredients together.

Put in quiche dish and press it down with your hands. Top with Hot Pepper Jelly.

Serve with crackers. Best if made a day in advance

Parmesan Chicken Wings

ELIZABETH & BILL JERRY
THE MOUSE TRAP

2 lbs. cut chicken wings

Spread wings in a large baking pan. Sprinkle generously with salt, pepper, thyme, oregano, paprika, and parmesan cheese.

Bake at 350 degrees for 30 to 45 minutes, stirring occasionally. More paprika and Parmesan cheese may be added about half way though.

Shrimp Paté
KATHI & JIM MITCHELL

4 7½ oz. can shrimp
½ cup butter, melted
⅓ cup mayonnaise
1 small onion, minced
2 tablespoons fresh lemon juice
Dash of Tabasco sauce

SAUCE
1 cup catsup
2 tablespoon horseradish
2 teaspoons fresh lemon juice
Blend all ingredients and refrigerate

Mash shrimp well and add onion. Pour butter over shrimp and onion. Add mayonnaise, lemon juice and Tabasco sauce. Mix and pack into a mold. Refrigerate for 3 hours. Unmold and pour sauce over paté.
  Serve with crackers. Makes 2½ cups.

Deviled Eggs
BETTY & DON BARTON

Boil Eggs, peel and cut in halves. Mash yolks and Add:

1 teaspoon vinegar
1 tablespoon prepared Dijon mustard and Durkees
2 tablespoons Dukes mayonnaise
¼ teaspoon paprika
1 tablespoon pickle relish (with juice squeeded out)
1 tablespoon finely grated Bermuda or white onion

Fill egg whites
Add ¼ jar caviar for garnish

Mexican Pie
BECKY HARPER

1 or 2 lbs. hamburger meat
1 onion
1 package Taco seasoning mix
1 16 oz. sour cream
1 jar salsa (16oz)
1 package Mexican or sharp cheddar cheese, shredded
1 can refried beans

Spread into bottom of pan. Pour sour cream over meat and spread evenly. Pour salsa and shredded cheese on top and bake at 350 degrees, uncovered, for 45 minutes to an hour.
  This is hot and spicy. Dip with Taco shells or your favorite cracker.

Ham Roll Ups
LYNNE MCCARTHA

1 package soft cream cheese
1 package Danish ham slices
1 jar picked okra

Let cream cheese soften to room temperature. Add garlic powder to taste. Pat ham slices dry and spread cream cheese over. Place picked okra on ham slice and roll to the size of a cigarette. Chill overnight, or for several hours. (Cover) Slice into small slices with electric knife.

Marinated Shrimp Medley

SUSIE & HEYWARD KING

2 lbs. medium shrimp, shelled and cooked
1 can artichoke hearts
1 can ripe olives
1 can mushroom caps
1 or 2 cups cherry tomatoes
(Use more or less of the ingredients you like best)

Mix all the above; pour Italian Dressing over and chill for several hours, or overnight.

Sausage Roll Ups

DONA W. FOWLER

2 lbs. country pork link sausage (Morty Pride)
3 cans crescent dinner rolls

Cook sausage, drain and cool. Cut into bite size pieces.
Open can of crescent rolls.
Unroll dough, separate into triangles, and spread hot spicy mustard on each triangle. Place 1 piece of sausage on a triangle and roll up.
Place all roll-ups on ungreased cookie sheet and bake at 350 degrees for 11 to 13 minutes or until golden brown.
Serves 24 roll-ups

Sugar and Spice Pecans

HANNALI & RED FURGUSON

1 egg white
1 tablespoon orange juice
1 cup sugar
¾ teaspoon salt
1 teaspoon cinnamon
1 lb. pecan halves

Beat egg white and orange juice until frothy, stir in sugar, salt, and cinnamon. Stir in pecans until completely coated. Spread on cookie sheet. Bake at 200 for 45 minutes. Stir every 15 minutes, remove when dry and toasty. Cool and store in airtight container.
Serves 4 cups

Basil Spread

MARY ELLA WRIGHT

Large clove of garlic
8 oz. cream cheese, room temperature
½ cup parmesan cheese
1 tablespoon sun dried tomato paste
1 tablespoon fresh dill (don't use dry)
4 oz. butter, room temperature
1 teaspoon lemon pepper
1 tablespoon sour cream

Blend garlic and fresh basil together in a food processor or blender. Add other ingredients. Add 1 tablespoon sour cream by hand. Refrigerate 1 hour.
Serve With hard bread or crackers. Also good over hot pasta. Thin with cream.

Blackeye Pea Cocktail Balls

FRANCES FULMER

1 15 oz. can black-eye peas, drained and mashed
2 tablespoons grated onion
1 egg, beaten
1 tablespoon salad oil
About 5 tablespoons all-purpose flour
Ground red pepper to taste
¼ teaspoon salt
¼ teaspoon pepper
¼ teaspoon sage
Salad oil for frying

Combine all ingredients, mixing well. Drop by round-ed teaspoons into hot oil; cook until browned. Drain on absorbent paper towels.
Yields about 2 dozen.

Cheddar and Bacon Log

CURTIS FRYE
COURTESY OF LAND 'O LAKES

1 (8 oz.) package of cream cheese, softened
3 tablespoons mayonnaise
⅛ teaspoon Worcestershire sauce
3 to 4 drops hot pepper sauce
8 ounces (2cups) Land 'O Lakes, Cheddar cheese, shredded
¼ cup crumbled crisply cooked bacon
2 tablespoons sliced green onions
1 cup chopped pecans, toasted

Beat cream cheese, mayonnaise. Worcestershire sauce and hot pepper sauce in large bowl on medium speed, scraping bowl often, until smooth (1 to 2 min-utes). Stir in cheese, bacon and green onions by hand. Cover; refrigerate at least 2 hours.

Form cheese mixture into log shape or cheese ball; roll in pecans to coat. Wrap in plastic food wrap; refrigerate until serving time.
Serve with crackers. Yields 1 log.

Cheese and Beef Roll-Ups

JIMMY KNIGHT
COURTESY OF LAND 'O LAKES

Prepare this appetizer ahead for hassle–free enter-taining.

1 (8 oz.) package cream cheese, softened
2 tablespoons prepared horseradish
5 (8-inch) flour tortillas
25 to 30 spinach leaves, stems removed

10 thin slices deli Italian roast beef
8 oz. (2cups) Land 'O Lakes American Process cheese, shredded

In small mixer bowl beat cream cheese and horseradish on medium speed, scraping bowl often, until smooth (1 to 2 minutes).

Spread about 3 tablespoons cream cheese mixture evenly on one tortilla. Arrange 5 to 6 spinach leaves over cream cheese. Place 2 slices roast beef over spinach. Sprinkle about ⅓ cup cheese over roast beef. Roll tortilla up tightly; wrap with plastic food wrap. Repeat with remaining tortillas. Refrigerate at least 4 hours or overnight
To serve Cut each tortilla into 1-inch slices. 30 appetizers

TOMMY ADDISON

A three-year letterman for the Gamecocks from 1955 to 1957, Tommy sent on to play for the Boston Patriots of the AFL for the leagues first eight years of existence.

He played in four Pro Bowls from 1961 to 1964.
Tommy served as first president of the AFL Players Associations. His 16 career interceptions rank among the leaders for professional linebackers.
Tommy was inducted into the South Carolina Hall of Fame last May.
Tommy was the only man to ever put fear in the heart of the legendary Corky Gaines. Tommy did not always fight fair.

Half-Time Jalapeño Roll-Ups
TOMMY ADDISON
COURTESY OF LAND 'O LAKES

Jalapeño Spread
1 cup Land 'O Lakes, sour cream
1 (8oz. package cream cheese, softened
8 oz. chunk Land 'O Lakes Jalapeño Process cheese, shredded (about 2 cups)
¼ cup chopped ripe olives
1 tablespoon sliced green onion
1 (2 oz.) jar diced pimiento, drained

ROLL-UPS
8 (8-inch) flour tortillas
8 lettuce leaves
8 think slices deli roast beef

Combine sour cream and cream cheese In small mixer bowl. Beat at medium speed, scraping bowl often, until smooth (1 to 2 minutes). Stir in all remaining jalapeño spread ingredients by hand.

Spread 3 heaping tablespoons jalapeno spread on each tortilla. Layer with lettuce leaf and roast beef. Roll up tightly. Wrap in plastic food wrap. Refrigerate at least 2 hours.

To Serve: unwrap; cut each roll-up in half.

Party Nibbler

JOHNNY GREGORY

1 cup salted cashews
1 cup salted peanuts
1 cup (1-inch square) cheese-flavored crackers
1 cup bite-size wheat chex cereal
1 cup bite-size pretzels
2 tablespoons freshly grated Parmesan cheese
¼ Land 'O Lakes butter, melted
1 teaspoon Worcestershire sauce
½ teaspoon celery salt
½ teaspoon garlic powder

Heat oven to 350 degrees. Combine cashews, peanuts, crackers, cereal, pretzels and Parmesan cheese in large bowl.

Combine all remaining ingredients in small bowl. Pour butter mixture over cereal mixture; toss to coat

Spread mixture onto ungreased 15 x 10 x 1-inch jelly roll pan. Bake, stirring occasionally, for 18 to 23 minutes or until lightly browned. Cool completely.

Spinich Balls

FRANCES FULMER

2 packages frozen chopped spinach (cook by directions-drain well)
1 8 oz. pkg. Pepperidge Farm herb stuffing
1 large onion minced
½ lb. butter, melted
½ cup Parmesan cheese
½ teaspoon garlic salt
½ teaspoon Accent or MSG

¼ teaspoon thyme
½ teaspoon black pepper

Mix all ingredients. Chill. Shape into balls. Bake 20 minutes at 350 degrees. These made be frozen uncooked. Thaw 20 minutes before baking. Yields 75-100.

Pickled Shrimp

RACHEL & GOVERNOR JIM HODGES

2 pounds of boiled shrimp, shelled and deveined
2 thinly sliced onions
2 cans of 4 oz. whole mushrooms
2 cans of 14 oz. artichoke hearts, drained and quartered
1 can of pitted black olives (6oz.),drained
1 cup of olive oil
1 cup of white wine vinegar
Salt and pepper to taste

Cream Cheese Salsa

JANICE MARTHERS

1 jar of salsa
2 packages of cream cheese
1-2 cups of shredded cheese

Allow cream cheese to come to room temperature. Mix all ingredients and serve with chips.

Lobster Paté

KATHI & JIM MITCHELL

1 8 oz. package cream cheese, softened
¼ cup dry white wine
½ teaspoon onion salt
½ teaspoon seasoned salt
⅛ teaspoon dill
1 ½ cups lobster meat, chopped

Beat cream cheese and wine until smooth and creamy. Blend in salts and dill; add lobster. Cover and refrigerate several hours or overnight to mellow. Yeilds 2½ cups.

Scott's "Hot and Spicy" BBQ Chicken Wings

JEAN & JIM POOLE

Scott's BBQ sauce can be purchased at any Food Lion Store

In a large pot place your chicken wings and cover with sauce (for a large pkg. of wings I usually use 2 bottles of sauce)
Warm sauce and chicken (do not cook) on burner for at least 30 minutes
Place chicken wings on hot grill and cook until golden brown.

Lynn Anderson's Nacho Mama's Salsa

LYNN ANDERSON & HOWARD HUGHES

28 oz. can whole tomatoes
1 medium onion (half of a large red one)
4 to 6 green chilies, chopped (or one small can of them, chopped)
2 cloves garlic, minced
1 tablespoon fresh Cilantro, chopped (absolutely NO MORE than 1 Tbsp.)
Salt if desired (½ tsp. recommended)
Freshly ground black pepper, to taste

Prepared in a blender on low speed
This is a good basic salsa for use as a dip, a condiment, or an ingredient in dozens of recipes. There are many variations to suit your taste. For example, use 3-4 fresh chopped tomatoes instead of the canned ones, or use 3-4 fresh chopped jalapeno peppers to make it hotter. I like to leave a small bowl of chopped jalapenos (or even a Habanera or two) next to my salsa for the wise guys who say: "That's not HOT!"
Country music superstar Lynn Anderson gave me her personal salsa recipe, but I've tweaked it a tad (in parentheses above) to perfection.

Deviled Eggs

ALICE FLANSBURG

Eggs do not have to be "fresh." Peel better if "older" Place eggs in pan—cover with cold water

Bring to Boil. Turn down heat—Simmer 17 minutes. Remove from heat. Drain.

Flood with cold water—change often to keep water cold. Peel Eggs. Place in refrigerator over night.

Chill dish to be used for serving

NEXT DAY

Cut in half length wise. Place whites on chilled dish. Place yolks in large mixing bowl. Mash with pastry blender. Add salt, pepper, prepared yellow mustard to taste, Kraft Miracle Whip salad dressing. Blend until fluffy. Fill egg whites with yolk mixture with teaspoon. Can be topped with paprika for color.

Can add to yolk mixture: Bacon bits, chopped onions, chives, chopped pickles, and chopped ripe olives.

Can garnish with: Sliced olives, sliced red pimento.

To be fancy—pipe yolk into whites with a cake decorating sleeve.

Tortilla Roll-Ups

HOWARD HUGHES

1 8 oz. bars Philadelphia Brand cream cheese, soften

1 package Ranch Salad Dressing mix (Hidden Valley preferred)

3 to 4 green onions, chopped

Red pepper, optional

2, 10 count package of large soft tortillas (don't even attempt this with the small ones)

Mix the cream cheese, ranch mix, and chopped green onions in a bowl.

Spread mixture thinly but completely and evenly over 1 side of tortilla (like doing pizza-hold the tortilla in one hand while spreading it with a table knife).

(If you use red pepper, very lightly sprinkle it over the tortilla prior to the next step). Roll tortillas fairly tightly and pinch the ends when complete.

Place them seam down in the refrigerator for several hours—long enough to let the tortillas stiffen and the insides chill—overnight will do nicely.

Then cut the rolls into about 1-inch sections (keep the pinched cut off ends to eat yourself, much as you would odd corner pieces from a brownie pan).

Serves 75 to 80 pieces. Goes especially good dipped in homemade Lynn Anderson's Nacho Mama's Salsa.

Trish's Deviled Eggs

TRISH NORRIS

8 eggs
mustard
mayonnaise
sweet pickle cubes

Cook the 8 eggs in boiling water for at least eight minutes or until eggs are cooked through. While eggs are hot to warm, crack the shells to remove the whole egg. Cut the egg in half and remove the cooked yellow yolk. Mash up the yolks in a bowl and then mix with a couple of squirts of mustard, one tablespoon of mayonnaise, and two tablespoons of sweet pickle cubes (not relish). Fill the yolk holes with this mixture. I pack in a deviled egg plastic container and store in the cooler until serving time.

BREADS

Pepperoni Bread ~ Susan and Brad Edwards

Banana-Apricot Nut Bread ~ Edith and Art Baker

Mushroom Bread ~ Nell and Ken Lester

Breakfast Pizza ~ Nell and Ken Lester

Broccoli Cornbread ~ Billy Canada

Sesame Cheese Muffins ~ Harold Green

Cheesy Herb Bread ~ Fred Zeiler

True Blue Muffins ~ Tommy Suggs

Southern Cornbread ~ Duce Staley

Gamecock Bread ~ Johnny Grambling

Quick Tea Ring ~ Dick Harris

Beer Muffins ~ Susan Watts

Spinach Cornbread ~ Kim and Jay Frye

Sally Lunn Bread ~ Margaret & Rudy Attaberry

Southern Spoon Bread ~ Margaret & Rudy Attaberry

Brenda Toast ~ Brenda Cheeks

BRAD EDWARDS

Brad is best remembered for his return interceptions for touchdowns against Clemson in both the 1986 and 1987 games. Brad went on from there to a ten year NFL career, playing for the Vickings, Redskins, Falcons and Packers. He played in Super Bowl XXVI. He is currently USC Associate Director of Athletics.

Pepperoni Bread
SUSAN & BRAD EDWARDS

2 loaves of frozen bread dough
1 stick of butter

1 teaspoon salt
1 teaspoon oregano
1 teaspoon basil
1 package of pepperoni (cut into quarters)
2 cups of provolone cheese (grated)
2 cups of mozzarella cheese (grated)

Thaw bread and using a rolling pin, roll dough into 9 by 13 rectangles. Melt butter and add seasoning to the butter. Brush bread with butter mixture according to desired amount, top with cheese and pepperoni. Beginning at the short end, roll bread and pinch sides to hold. Bake according to bread package directions. Allow to cool and then slice and serve.

Banana Apricot Nut Bread
EDITH & ART BAKER

2 cups self-rising flour
1 cup sugar
1 egg
½ cups dried apricots, chopped
¾ cup ripe banana, mashed
½ cup milk
½ cup chopped nuts, pecans or walnuts

In a large bowl stir together flour, sugar, salt, apricots and nuts. Combine banana, milk and egg, mix with dry ingredients. Pour into a 9 x 5 inch loaf pan. Cook at 350 degrees for 1 hour. Let cool in pan for 10 minutes. Remove loaf out of pan. Cool on rack.

Mushroom Bread

NELL & KEN LESTER

1 loaf French bread
1 pound sliced Swiss cheese
2 sticks of butter
1 large jar of mushrooms
1 tablespoon dry mustard
½ teaspoons lemon juice
1 teaspoon seasoned salt

Put the butter, mushrooms, dry mustard, lemon juice and seasoned salt in the pan over heat until butter is melted.

Cut bread and stuff cheese in slices. Spoon melted mixture over bread. Wrap in foil and bake at 350 degrees for 45 minutes

Breakfast Pizza

NELL & KEN LESTER

1 pound bulk pork sausage
1 package (8) refrigerated crescent rolls
1 cup frozen loose-pack harsh brown potatoes, thawed
1 cup shredded sharp cheddar cheese (4 oz.)
8 eggs
¼ cup milk
½ teaspoon salt
½ teaspoon pepper
2 tablespoons grated Parmesan cheese

Cook sausage until brown; drain. Separate crescent dough into 8 triangles. Place in ungreased 12 oz.

Pizza Pan, with points toward the center. Press over bottom and up sides to form a crust, seal perforations. Spoon sausage over crust. Sprinkle with potatoes. Top with cheese.

In large bowl, beat eggs, milk, salt, pepper and pour into the crust. Sprinkle parmesan over all. Bake at 350 degrees for 25 minutes.
Servings: 6 to 8

Broccoli Cornbread

BILLY CANADA

1 – 10 oz. pkg. Chopped broccoli
1 stick butter
6 oz. cottage cheese
1 large onion chopped fine
4 eggs
1 teaspoon salt
1 box Jiffy cornbread mix

In a 2 qt. pan slowly melt butter. Add broccoli and cottage cheese. Stir until smooth, add other ingredients. Pour in a 9 x 13 greased pan. Bake 25 to 30 minutes at 400 degrees.

HAROLD GREEN

Led the team in rushing three consecutive years (1987-89)....ranks third all time at USC in rushing yards with 3,005.

Played for NFL's Cincinnati Bengal from 1990-1996, St Louis Rams in 1996-97 and for the Falcons 1997-98...His 33 career touchdowns ties him with George Rogers for the school record. He is in the Athletic Hall of Fame.

Sesame Cheese Muffins

HAROLD GREEN

COURTESY OF KATHI MITCHELL

1½ cups Bisquick biscuit mix
¾ cup grated sharp cheddar cheese
¼ cup minced onions
1 egg, well beaten
½ cup milk
1 Tablespoon sesame seeds, toasted

Sauté onions in the butter until transparent. Mix Bisquick mix and ½ cup cheese together. Combine egg, milk and onion. Add all at once to Bisquick mixture and beat vigorously for 30 seconds. Fill well greased muffin tins ⅔ full. Sprinkle tops with some of the grated cheese and sesame seeds. Bake at 400 degrees for 12 to 15 minutes.
Servings: 12 Servings

FRED ZEILER

Fred caught 146 passes for 1,876 yards during his Gamecock career from 1967 to 1969. He was inducted into the USC Athletic Hall of Fame in 1995.

Cheesy Herb Bread

FRED ZEILER

COURTESY OF KATHI MITCHELL

1 loaf French bread
1 clove garlic, minced
1 teaspoon marjoram leaves
½ cup softened butter
¼ cup finely chopped parsley
1 cup Parmesan cheese

Slice bread into 1–inch slices. In a small bowl combine all but cheese and mix well. Spread mixture on bread. Sprinkle with parmesan cheese. Wrap in foil and bake at 400 degrees for 20 minutes. Unwrap and bake an additional 5 minutes. Rewrap until ready to serve.
Servings: 8

TOMMY SUGGS

Shares the record for the most touchdown passes in one game. Tommy threw for 4,916 yards and 34 touchdowns...all of those marks were once records and now ranks second behind Todd Ellis. More importantly he never lost to Clemson. Tommy is in his 32nd year as a color analyst for the Gamecock football network.

True Blue Muffins

TOMMY SUGGS
COURTESY OF KATHI MITCHELL

1¼ cup flour, sifted
2 teaspoons baking powder
½ cup sugar
½ teaspoon salt

¼ cup melted butter
1 egg
¼ cup milk
¾ cup blueberries
¼ lemon juice

Cream butter and sugar. Add eggs. Add flour and baking powder alternating with milk and lemon juice. Fold in berries carefully. Bake at 400 degrees for 20 minutes.
Servings: 12 muffins

DUCE STALEY

In his senior year, 1996, Duce led the SEC in rushing with 1,116 yards, earning first team All-SEC honors.

Drafted 3rd by the Philadelphia Eagles, he begins his seventh NFL season this fall. Duce has rushed for 4,344 career yards with 17 touchdowns. He has 239 career receptions with eight touchdowns. In just six years he is already the fourth all-time leading rusher in Eagle history.

As a Columbia, South Carolina native he still makes his home here.

Southern Cornbread

DUCE STALEY
COURTESY OF KATHI MITCHELL

2 cups buttermilk
2 eggs
1 teaspoon baking soda
1 teaspoon salt
1½ cups cornmeal
3 tablespoons bacon grease

Put 3 tablespoons bacon grease in iron skillet and heat slightly. While grease is getting hot, mix all the other ingredients together. Pour batter into hot skillet. Bake at 400 degrees until firm, about 40 minutes.

Gamecock Bread

JOHNNY GRAMBLING
COURTESY OF KATHI & JIM MITCHELL

2 tablespoons softened butter
¼ cup hot water
½ cup orange juice
1½ tablespoons freshly grated orange rind
1 egg
1 cup sugar
2 cups flour
1 teaspoon baking powder
½ teaspoon salt
¼ teaspoon baking soda
1 cup fresh raspberries, or frozen, well drained

Combine butter, water, orange juice and rind in a bowl. Add egg and mix well. Add dry ingredients and fold in raspberries by hand. Bake at 325 degrees in greased 9 x 5 inch baking pan for 1 hour and 10 minutes. Cool on rack.

JOHNNY GRAMBLING

South Carolina's first to surpass 2,000 careers passing yards...Passed for 2,007 yards and 18 touchdowns, both career records at the time. Threw for 227 yards against Wake Forest in 1953...Threw four T.D.'s in the first half against Furman in 1951. Played for the Ottawa Roughridgers in the Canadian League in 1954, but his professional career was cut short by military service in the Korean War.

DICK HARRIS

Made all ACC and first team All American in 1971. Dickie was the most exciting kick returner in the history of the school. His 162 punt, kick off, and interception returns netted him 2,767 yards and six touchdowns.

Dickie had two returns of more than 90 yards in one game. A kickoff of 96 yards and a pass interception return of 94 yards against Georgia in 1970. He returned a punt 96 yards against North Carolina that same year. He played 10 years of pro football in the Canadian League. He is a member of University's Hall of Fame.

Quick Tea Ring

DICK HARRIS
COURTESY OF KATHI MITCHELL

¼ cup brown sugar
1½ tablespoon cream
¼ cup melted butter
¼ cup chopped pecans
2 cans refrigerated biscuits
3 tablespoons melted butter
1 teaspoon ground cinnamon
½ cup sugar

Mix brown sugar, cream, melted butter and nuts. Place in bottom of 1½ quart salad mold. Dip each biscuit in melted butter, then in cinnamon sugar mixture. Bake at 425 degrees for 20 to 25 minutes.

Beer Muffins

SUSAN WATTS

1 cup Bisqick
1 tablespoon sugar
4 ounces beer

Mix and spoon into greased muffin tins. Bake in 400 degrees oven for 20 minutes. Quick and easy, yet delicious.
Servings: Makes 6

JAY FRYE

Jay is a third generation Gamecock. His father, Jerry, was a co-captain of USC's 1960 team. His grandfather, Sarge, was grounds keeper for the Athletic Department for 43 years. Serge was so good at his trade; he could grow grass on Frank Howard's head.

Jay was a special team's player for the Gamecock's in 1983-84. Currently he is the head football coach at Richland N. E. High School in Columbia.

Spinach Cornbread

KIM & JAY FRYE

1 10 oz. frozen chopped spinach
1 large onion, chopped
½ cup butter
4 eggs, beaten
1 cup cottage cheese
1 teaspoon salt
Jiffy cornbread mix

Cook and drain spinach. Sauté onion in butter until transparent. Combine all ingredients and pour into lightly greased 9 x 9 inch pan. Bake at 375 degrees for 50 minutes or until golden.
Servings: 9

Sally Lund Bread

MARGARETE & RUDY ATTABERRY

2 cups sifted flour
3 teaspoons baking powder
½ teaspoon salt1 egg beaten
1 cup milk
½ cup milk
½ cup shortening
¼ cup sugar

Sift flour, baking powder and salt together. Combine egg and milk. Cream shortening and sugar together and add flour alternately with liquid mixture. Place in greased loaf or muffin pan. Bake at 375 for 30 minutes.
Servings: Makes 1 loaf or 12 muffins

Southern Spoon Bread

MARGARETE & RUDY ATTABERRY

2 cups boiling water
1 cup white corn meal
1 teaspoon salt
1 tablespoon shortening
1 cup milk
2 eggs, separated

Mix water, cornmeal, salted shortening. Cool. Add milk and beaten egg yolks; mix well. Fold in stiffly beaten egg whites. Pour into greased baking dish. Bake at 400 degrees for 30 to 40 minutes.
Servings: Serves 6 to 9

Brenda's Toast

BRENDA CHEEK
COURTESY OF CHARLIE HAWKINS

16 oz of cream cheese (soft)
2 cups mayonnaise
3 teaspoon grated onion
6 green onions (spring onions)
½ teaspoon paprika
2 cups parmesan cheese
Cobblestone French bread rolls

Mix all the above except the parmesan cheese.
Slice rolls in bite size pieces and spread the mix on one side. Roll in the parmesan cheese. Make it thick. Put on a cookie sheet and freeze. When frozen put in a bag and seal. Return to freezer. Take out of freezer the amount you want and cook at 350 degrees until brown. About 3 or 4 minutes.
This is good to serve with salads, soup etc.
Often I garnish with jalapeño pepper or olives and whatever I have.

CHILIS & SOUPS

MRS. WEEMS O. BASKIN, JR.

Wife of Big Weemie Baskin and mother of Little Weemie Baskin. She was the first lady of coaches for the Gamecocks from 1948 to 1967.

Mack Baskin's Easy Chili
WEEMIE BASKIN

Small container of sour cream
8 oz. package shredded sharp cheddar cheese
1 1 oz. package of corn chips
1 lb. ground beef
1 12-14 oz. can of tomato soup
1 12-14 oz. can of kidney beans
2 tablespoons chili powder
½ cup of diced onions

Saute ground beef with onions on medium heat until done. Stir. Add soup and beanbs, chili powder. Stir. Top off with sour cream and cheese for dip or servings. Dip and eat with corn chips.
Servings: 6

ROY BEASLEY

Roy and the boys have been terrorizing the citizens of Barnwell County for over forty years. They are not mafia or Al Queda, as they seldom use explosives. Their general conduct is usually bad enough to achieve their respective goals. When Roy submitted this recipe I was afraid not to use it.

Catfish Stew
ROY BEASLEY
KNIFE, ALLEY CAT, FAT CAT, & FLASH

6 gallon deep fry cooker
10 lbs. onions
10 lbs potatoes
15 lbs catfish

Put all the above in layers, then add water 3 inches below full. Light the fire and have a 32 oz. drink of Early Times. Start telling lies. Refill your drink every

30 minutes. When lies run out, start playing Iyer's poker, pitching quarters to a line, and finally telling stories about women you have known. Cook for 6 hrs. or until Early Times has run out. Next, get two friends to dump stew into swift running stream. Have the third friend help you to his car and let him drive you home. This is particularly important as I didn't follow my own recipe in 1963 and ended up running my car into a parked train

Lou Holtz Chili
COACH LOU HOLTZ

1¼ pounds of ground sirloin
2 cloves garlic
Olive oil
3 tablespoons chili powder
1 – (15½ oz.) can dark red kidney beans
1 – (46 oz.) can V8 juice
28 oz. can crushed tomatoes
1 12 oz. can tomato paste
1 – 12 oz. can water

Brown garlic lightly in olive oil. Remove garlic and set aside. Brown sirloin in garlic flavored oil. Once the meat is browned, return garlic to meat. Add all the remaining ingredients except kidney beans. Simmer to desired thickness (about 1½ hours). Add kidney beans during the last half hour of cooking.

We have a lot liquid with ours as Lou likes a small amount of cooked elbow macaroni at the bottom of bowl and chili over (macaroni absorbs some of the liquid). If desired sprinkle with shredded cheddar cheese and/ or chopped onion.

Steak Sauce Chili
JOE BRAMLETT

2 – 2.5 lbs. Top Round with excess fat removed and cubed into 1 inch squares
3 large onions
4 cloves of fresh garlic
1 28 oz. can of whole tomatoes halved
1 16 oz. can of tomato sauce

CONTINUED

1 6 oz. can tomato paste
¾ cup Heinz 57 sauce
¾ cup A-1 sauce

Cook beef cubes in pressure cooker with appropriate amount of water for your pressure cooker about 30 minutes or until cubes are beginning to flake. While beef is cooking, brown garlic and onion mixture in olive oil (approx. 4 tablespoons), until onions and garlic are golden brown. In a 4-5 quart pot add all of the ingredients, and place on stove at low to medium heat. Cook with lid on pot, stirring frequently so as not to allow sticking. Chili should cook for 2 to 3 hours or until cubes of beef are falling completely apart.
Servings: 8 to 10

Broccoli Soup
TERRY FLOYD

1 pkgs. Frozen broccoli
3 cups chicken broth
½ cup chopped onion
½ cup white pepper
4 tables. Melted margarine
5 Tbls. flour
1 carton, half and half

Simmer broccoli until tender. Sauté onions in margarine. Blend melted margarine with flour. Pour half and half over this. Mix with top ingredients and serve with corn dodgers or saltines.

HOOTIE JOHNSON

The Chairman of Augusta National was a three year South Carolina football letterman.

Hootie played in the shadows of Bishop Strickland and Steve Wadiak, two of the greatest running backs in Gamecock history. But as a blocker he excelled. He won the Jacobs Blocking Trophy in his senior year.

At age 34, Johnson became the youngest bank president ever in South Carolina.

Hot Dog Sauce
PIERRINE & HOOTIE JOHNSON

2 lb. lean ground beef
2 cups chopped onion

¼ cup water
8 oz. ketchup
1 teaspoon Worcestershire
2 teaspoons Heinz 57
1 tablespoon yellow mustard

Brown the ground beef until crumbly, add onions and water. Add remaining ingredients. Cover and cook on low heat until meat and onions are done. Drain off fat, if necessary, and serve over hot dogs.

Hungarian Goulash Soup
HANNALI & RED FURGUSON

2 onions, chopped
2 garlic cloves. minced
¼ cup vegetable oil
3 tbsp. hot Hungarian paprika
1½ lb. beef chuck, chopped fine
1 tbsp. caraway seeds
3½ cup brown stock or canned beef broth
1 large tomato, peeled, seeded, and chopped
1 tsp. dried marjoram

Cook onions and garlic in oil over moderate heat. 6 to 8 minutes on until golden. Remove from heat and stir in paprika. Add beef, caraway seeds, stock, salt and pepper to taste and simmer for 1 hour or until beef is almost tender. Add tomato and marjoram, and simmer for 10 minutes. Add salt and pepper to taste and ladle into heated bowls.
Servings: 8 cups

Carroll's Chili
JOHN CARROLL

3 lb. London broil roast (have your butcher remove all the fat and grind the meat 2 times.)
1 can (32oz.) Hunts diced tomatoes
3 cans (15oz.) Hunts seasoned diced tomato sauce for chili
2 cans (15½ oz.) Hanover Dark red kidney beans
1 can (10oz.) Rotelle original diced tomatoes and green chilies
1 large onion, chopped
1 green pepper, chopped
1 teaspoon garlic, minced
1 healthy dash of chili powder
Salt and pepper to taste.

Brown onion and bell pepper with meat. Drain the grease. Add all other ingredients. Cook on low heat for two hours.

J.R.'s World Famous Oyster Stew
J. R. WILBURN

1½ Tablespoons flour
1½ teaspoons salt
2 dashes of Tabasco sauce
1 dash of garlic salt
2 tablespoons cold water
1 pint Chesapeake Bay oysters (standard) and their liquor
¼ cup butter
1 qt. half and half

CONTINUED

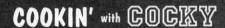
In medium saucepan, combine first 5 ingredients into smooth paste. Add oysters and butter and simmer mixture over verylow heat for 5 minutes until oysters edge curl. Stirring gently.

In separate saucepan scald half and half. Pour in oyster mixture, remove from heat, cover and let set for 15 minutes. Dash with paprika and serve with oyster crackers.

Servings: 3 or 4

Garnish with diced tomatoes, chopped scallions, slices black olives, shredded cheese,

Eat with Tortillas warmed. The scoop kind.

Serves 4

White Chicken Chili

STUART WHATLEY

1 tablespoons olive oil
1½ cups onions, chopped
3 cloves garlic, finely chopped
2 teaspoons dried oregano
1½ teaspoons ground cumin
½ teaspoon powdered ginger
1½ cups chicken broth
½ cups dry white wine
1 bay leaf, broken in half
2 cups chicken or turkey, cooked and chopped
2 cups white beans, cooked and drained (we used Great Northern)
2 jalapeno pepper, minced
1½ cups Monterey Jack cheese, grated
½ teaspoons black pepper
Salt to taste

Sauté onions in olive oil, add garlic, oregano, cumin and ginger. Sauté for about 5 minutes. Mash half of the beans and add to the broth, wine, bay leaf, and chicken. Then add pepper cheese and salt and pepper and the rest of the beans.

DIPS & SAUCES

Virtually fat-free Yummy Bean Dip ~ Ginger and Mike McGee

Sweet Vidalia Dip ~ Renee & Punky Holler

Ham and Cheese Dip ~ Edith & Art Baker

Shrimp Dip ~ Robbie & Sam Vickers

Black Bean Salsa Dip ~ Betsy & Ronnie Collins

Shrimp Dip ~ Gwen Adams

Shrimp Dip ~ Peggy & Joe Pinner

Blue cheese Shrimp Dip ~ Cathy & Gerald Sease

Broccoli Dip ~ Jan & Alvin Roof

Avocado Crab Dip ~ Kathi & Jimmy Mitchell

California Mound Dip ~ Phyllis Cox

Refried Bean / Taco Dip ~ Carol & Bob Fulton

Jeanne's Crab Dip ~ Al Johnson

The Kahuna Dip ~ Myrna & Preacher Whitner

Crowd Pleaser Dip ~ Martha Seay

Dill Dip ~ Betsy & Ronnie Collins

Bacon Dip ~ Pam Harrison

Sausage Dip ~ Eaton Marchant

Taco Dip ~ Trish Norris

Layered Mexican Dip ~ Norma & Harold Steele

Sausage Dip ~ Jenny Thompson

Mexican Dip ~ Jill & Jeff Grantz

Jezebel Sauce ~ Bill Jones

Garnet & Black Bean Dip ~ Augusta & King Dixon

B.B.Q. Sauce ~ Brother Pitts

Cream Cheese, Pecan, Pineapple, Date Spread ~ Cheryl & Ken Wheat

Central Market's Poblano-Cilantro Pesto ~ Austin Texas

7 Layer Mexican Dip ~ Cathy Huggins

Virtually Fat-Free Yummy Bean Dip

GINGER & MIKE MCGEE

2 cans of black beans, drained
2 cans of white shoepeg corn, drained
1 each (diced)-sweet green, yellow and red pepper
5 pencil onions, sliced thin
2-3 stalks celery, chopped
1 large bottle of salsa
Salt and pepper to taste

*Mix all ingredients. Refrigerate overnight.
Serve with tortilla chips. Enjoy!*

PUNKY HOLLER

As my good friend and attorney for over 40 years, I'm not quite sure if he's gotten me out of more trouble than he's gotten me in.

Punky played in the NFL for three years with the Green Bay Packers and the Pittsburg Steelers. He played another two years in the Canadian League with Toronto.

Sweet Vidalia Dip

RENEE & PUNKY HOLLER

2 cups Vidalia onions, chopped
2 cups sharp cheese, shredded
2 cups Hellmann's mayonnaise, no substitute
1 tomato, chopped
Parsley

Mix first 3 ingredients. Put into pie dish. Garnish with tomato and parsley. Bake 350 degrees, until bubbles. Serve hot with triscuits or wheat thins

Ham and Cheese Dip

EDITH & ART BAKER

1 (5oz.) jar pimento cheese spread
1 (2¼ oz.) can deviled ham
1 teaspoon onion, minced
½ cup salad dressing
2 teaspoons parsley, minced
4 drops of Tabasco sauce

Blend the above ingredients with electric mixer. Chill.

SAM VICKERS

Athletes come in all sizes, shapes and colors. Many are immature, reckless and irresponsible. Sam Vickers was never one of the above. He came to school a mature and serious student, fully aware of his capabilities and limitation.

His intelligence and leadership qualities should have made him our starting quarterback, but he never was because...well...he kept getting knocked-out. Then you had to play both offense and defense which meant you had to make tackles. Sixty percent of the time when Sam made a tackle he was rendered unconscious. He was the only player I have ever known to be knocked out twice in the same game.

But it must have done no permanent damage, because Sam is now Chairman of the Board and CEO of Design Container Corporation of Jacksonville, Fl. That does business all over the world. He is on the Board of Directors of the South Financial Group. He was chairman of the Federal Reserve Board for six years. He also owns the finest collection of Florida art in the world. That's not bad for a boy who couldn't stay awake throughout a full football game.

Mama Vickers Shrimp Dip
ROBBIE & SAM VICKERS

1 8 oz. container sour cream
1 8 oz. package cream cheese
3 tablespoons mayonnaise
1 can tiny shrimp, drained
Hot sauce to taste

Combine all ingredients. Dip potato chips and enjoy!

Black Bean Salsa Dip
BETSY & RONNIE COLLINS

2 cans black beans, rinsed and drained
1 can corn, drained
1 bunch green onions, chopped
2 tablespoons lime juice
2 tablespoons vegetable oil
1 can Rotel tomatoes and green chilies

Combine all. Chill one hour. Serve with taco chips.

Shrimp Dip
GWEN ADAMS

1 pint Hellmann's mayonnaise, no substitute
1 small grated onion, to taste, 1½ tbsp.
1 small canned shrimp

Drain shrimp. Soak overnight in 2 tablespoons of lemon juice in refrigerator.

CONTINUED

Drain shrimp; add 2 more tablespoons lemon juice. Mix mayonnaise, shrimp and a dash of Worchestershire sauce and onion. Refrigerate. Serve with favorite cracker, club or whole wheat, etc.

they have two sons and four grandchildren. Joe was and is an institution unto himself and his positive attitude is infectious. What a wonderful and gentle man.

JOE PINNER

Joe was born in 1935 in Morehead City, North Carolina. He has been in radio and television since 1950 and with WIS TV since 1963 where he has served as Weather Man, Verity/Talk Show and Children Show Host and Commercial Announcer. Joe was the recipient of countless awards including The National 1967 George Foster Peabody award for the "Mr. Knozit" Children's Show which aired for 38 years.

He has been married to Peggy for 47 years and

Shrimp Dip
PEGGY & JOE PINNER

2 cups sour cream
¼ cup of lemon juice
1 8 oz. package cream cheese
1 pack Good Season's Dressing mix
1 pack frozen cooked shrimp

In mixing bowl combine sour cream, lemon juice, cream cheese and dressing mix. Blend to smooth paste. Chop shrimp into small bits and fold into paste mixture. Refrigerate until ready to serve.

Hi "Hawk" & "Dove"—Here it is—simple but simply simple and simply scrumptious!!!

We have had this recipe for more than forty years.

Blue Cheese Shrimp Dip
CATHY & GERALD SEASE

1 lb. peeled, cleaned shrimp; can use frozen
¼ lb. blue cheese or Gorgonzola cheese, crumbled
3 tablespoons olive oil
¼ cup finely chopped onions
1 teaspoon Worcestershire sauce
4 cups seasoned water. Season w/Crab Boil or Greek Seasoning

Bring seasoned water to boil; Even if frozen shrimp is already cooked, boil for approx. 5 minutes in seasoned water; drain well. Meanwhile, place cheese in microwave for 3 seconds until softened; okay if it melts. Combine softened cheese, onions, Worcestershire sauce and blend well. Combine drained shrimp and olive oil. Add cheese mixture and stir until coated. Refrigerate

Serve with Bremner crackers—or any unsalted cracker

Shrimp can be frozen and thawed for later use. If used for tailgating, keep cool during game.

Broccoli Dip
JAN & ALVIN ROOF

1 package of frozen chopped broccoli
½ teaspoon salt
1 onion, chopped
1 tablespoon butter
1 can cream of mushroom soup
1 teaspoon Worcestershire sauce
Tabasco sauce
Cayenne pepper
1 roll of garlic cheese
6 oz can of chopped mushrooms, drained
¾ cup of slivered almonds

Cook broccoli as directed then drain. Sauté onion in butter. Add soup, Worcestershire sauce, and little Tabasco and cayenne pepper. Then 1 roll of garlic cheese and mushrooms, drained, and then add almonds. Heat until cheese melts. Keep warm in a chafing dish. Serve with Frito Scoops.

Avacado-Crab Dip
KATHI & JIMMY MITCHELL

1 large avocado, mashed
1 tablespoon fresh lemon juice
2 tablespoons grated onion
1 teaspoon Worcestershire sauce
1 8 oz. package cream cheese, softened
½ cup sour cream
½ teaspoon salt
1 7½ can crabmeat, drained and flaked

Mix mashed avocado with lemon juice, onion and Worcestershire sauce. Stir in cream cheese, sour cream and salt. Add crabmeat and mix thoroughly. Serve with tortilla chips.
Makes 2 cups

California Mound Dip
PHYLLIS COX
COURTESY OF SUSIE KING

2 cups refried beans
2 medium avocados, mashed, with lemon juice
1 cup sour cream mixed with ½ pkg. Taco seasoning
½ cup Monterey Jack cheese, grated
½ cup cheddar cheese, grated
½ cup onion, chopped
½ cup tomatoes, chopped, with 1 teaspoon Tabasco
½ cup black olives, chopped
½ cup cilantro or parsley, chopped

Layer all ingredients. Serve with tortilla chips or nachos.

Refried Bean / Taco Dip
CAROL & BOB FULTON

1 can of refried beans
1 package of taco seasoning
1 small can of green chilies
1 small can of black olives
About ½ pound Monterey Jack cheese, grated
1 medium tomato
8 oz. sour cream

Mix refried beans and seasoning. Chop onions, chilies, olives, and tomato.

In a 9 x 11 dish spread bean/seasoning mixture on bottom. Layer chilies, olives, onion, tomato and sour cream. Sprinkle cheese on top layer. Serve with large, study corn chips (nacho style).

Jeanne's Crab Dip
AL JOHNSON

3 8oz. cream cheese, softened
1½ cup Crabmeat
2 tablespoons Onions, finely chopped
1½ teaspoons Worcestershire sauce
2 tablespoons mayonnaise

Mix all ingredients in large bowl. Place in pie plate and sprinkle with paprika. Bake at 350 degrees until it puffs and browns. Approx. 20 to 25 minutes. Serve warm with Carr's Common Crackers

The Kahuna Dip
MYRNA & PREACHER WHITNER

5 cups (1¼ lb.) extra sharp Cheddar cheese, grated
2 jars pimentos (4 oz. each) drained and mashed
1 jar (16oz.) Hot Thick and Chunky Salsa, to taste
3 tablespoons mayonnaise (approx.)
Black pepper, to taste
Tabasco sauce, if needed

Mix together all ingredients. Serve with scoops or Tortilla chips. This freezes well.
Makes approx. 5 cups

Crowd Pleaser Dip

MARTHA SEAY
ATO COOKBOOK

2 light cream cheese packages
2 tablespoons curry
1 jar Major Greys Chutney
1 lb. cooked-chopped bacon
1 can smoked almonds- optional
Green scallions, chopped fine

Mix cream cheese and curry together. Spread in container-pie dish works nicely. Spread chutney on top. Sprinkle chopped bacon on top. Sprinkle almonds and onion on top. Serve with big Fritos or crackers.

Dill Dip

BETSY & RONNIE COLLINS

1 cup sour cream
1 cup mayonnaise
1 tablespoon dill weed
1 tablespoon dry parsley
1 tablespoon dry chives
1 tablespoon dry minced onion
1 teaspoon seasoned salt

Combine all and chill. Delicious with chips, vegetables, etc.

Bacon Dip

PAM HARRISON
COURTESY OF SUSAN WATTS

24 ounces sour cream
2 cups shredded sharp cheddar cheese
1 jar Real bacon bits
1 package dry ranch mix

Mix well and refrigerate overnight. Serve with Tostitos.

Sausage Dip

EATON MARCHANT

1 package Jimmy Dean hot sausage
1 can of Ro-Tel tomatoes and green chilies
8 oz. Cream cheese

Brown sausage. Add tomatoes and cream cheese. Warm. Serve with Fritos. This recipe was given to me by my good friend Gus Hoffmeyer. It is easy to make and is great as a tailgating dish

Taco Dip

TRISH NORRIS

1 can refried beans
½ envelope Taco Seasoning Mix
1 avocado, mashed and mixed with 1 tablespoon
mayonnaise and 1 tablespoon lemon juice
4 oz. French onion dip
1 small can sliced ripe olives
1 cup chopped fresh tomatoes
8 oz. grated Monterey Jack or cheddar cheese

Combine refried beans and taco seasoning. Spread in a square rectangle plastic container with a lid. Then mix the avocado mixture with the French onion dip and spread on top of the refried beans. Spread the sour cream on top of the avocado mixture. Top with olives, tomatoes and then the cheese.

Serve with tortilla chips. Store in the cooler until serving time. My grown children require the taco dip at every tailgate.

Layered Mexican Dip

NORMA & HAROLD STEELE

MEAT
½ lb. ground beef (sirloin if preferred)
½ teaspoon chili powder
1-15 oz. refried beans
1-8 oz. tomato sauce
1 package taco seasoning mix
1 small onion, finely chopped
½ green pepper
½ teaspoon dry mustard

LAYERS
1 cup sour cream
2 cups shredded lettuce
2 cups shredded cheddar cheese

Brown meat, drain. Add all other ingredients to drained meat. Spread in 10 inch oblong ungreased dish. Layer in the following order. The meat, spread sour cream, sprinkle lettuce, add cheddar cheese. Warm in oven long enough to melt cheese.

Sausage Dip

JENNY THOMPSON

1 lb. Jimmy Dean Hot sausage
1 8 oz. block of cream cheese
1 10 oz. can of Rotel Diced Tomastoes
   and green chilies

Brown sausage, drain grease. Add cream cheese and melt slowly into meat. Add Tomatoes. Heat until bubbly. Pour into a crock pot to keep warm. Serve with Tostitoes.

JEFF GRANTZ

Second team All American in 1975. One of only three Gamecocks with more than 5,000 yards of total offense. An equally outstanding baseball player. He played shortstop and second base...Jeff played on three NCAA play off clubs, including the 1975 team that advanced to the finals of the College World Series.

Because of my playing and broadcasting career I didn't get to see Carolina play for 15 years, but I was in the stands in 1975 when Jeff threw for 5 touchdowns and ran for another as he led Carolina to a 56-20 win over Clemson.

CONTINUED

It was, perhaps, the greatest performance I have ever seen.

He is just as competitive today, but it's on the golf course.

Mexican Dip

JILL & JEFF GRANTZ

8 oz. block softened cream cheese
10 oz. hot dog chili sauce
8 oz. Monterey Jack cheese (shredded)

Spread cream cheese in bottom of casserole dish. Spread hot dog chili on top. Sprinkle with shredded cheese. Bake at 350 degrees for 20-254 minutes until cheese bubbles. Serve with tortilla chips.

BILL JONES

I've met a lot of people in my life, but Bill Jones doesn't remind me of none of them. I've known Bill for nearly 50 years and he hasn't changed one bit. His motto was and is, "If it ain't fun don't do it." He is always "up". "If he isn't having fun he'll find a way to reverse that in short order.

Bill was a fraternity brother and the head-cheerleader for the Gamecocks 1957-1960. He was also a long distance runner on the track team and a long distance swimmer.

Bill, Mr. Consistency, finished dead last in every event he ever participated in during his four years at Carolina...But, he never quit in a race...never. Sometimes he finished links behind the leaders, sometimes it was minutes.

During his senior year Bill was informed by someone in the Athletic department that he had earned a USC Letter. He went through the "Block C" initiation and to this day he proudly wears his Block C ring.

He never learned which coach gave him his letter. He was so proud, but too embarrassed to ask.

There are no pictures of Bill Jones to be found. The cameraman took pictures of the winners and left before Bill got to the finish line.

Jezebel Sauce

BILL JONES

1 (16oz.) jar apple jelly
1 (16oz.) jar pineapple preserves
1 (5oz.) jar horseradish
1 (1½ oz.) can dry mustard
Cream Cheese
Assorted crackers

Mix first four ingredients cover and refrigerate. Spread over cream cheese and serve with assorted crackers. Also good with meatballs, sliced ham or sausage.

Stores indefinitely in individual small jars in the refrigerator.
Yields: 3½ cups

Garnet and Black Bean Dip
AUGUSTA & KING DIXION

½ purple onion, chopped small
2 cans black beans (Progresso)
1 can shoepeg corn (Green Giant)
2 or 3 chopped tomatoes
1 avacado chopped

B.B.Q. Sauce
BROTHER PITTS

¼ cup oil
1 onion
3 tbs. mustard
3 tbs. Worcestershire
¼ cup lemon juice
8 oz. tomato sauce

½ cup brown sugar
Tabasco, to taste
½ cup water

Cook onion until soft in oil. Add all the rest of the above ingredients.

Foot note: I have used this BBQ recipe for over 40 years with tremendous success. It is simple to concoct and is equally enjoyable with poultry, beef or pork. Charlie (Old Timer) says it is delicious with possum, coon, or "cooter", (the turtle kind).

Cream Cheese, Pecan, Pineapple, Date Spread
CHERY & KEN WHEAT

1 8 oz. package cream cheese
1 small can crushed pineapple
1 cup chopped dates
1 cup pecan pieces

Soften cream cheese, mix with other ingredients. Serve as a dip or spread.

Best with Wheat thins (can be placed in food processor, but appearance is not as appealing. Can be served in scooped out pineapple). Serve with Wheat Thins.

Central Market's Poblano-Cilantro Pesto

AUSTIN, TEXAS
COURTESY OF D.J. & SCOTT KYLE

This unique pesto is fabulous served in or as a topping for fajitas or quesadillas.

4 poblano chili peppers
¾ cup freshly grated Parmesan cheese
1½ cup fresh cilantro
1/4 cup chopped walnuts (I like pecans)
¾ cup olive oil
3 garlic cloves
3 tablespoons fresh lime juice
1 teaspoon salt

Place peppers on an aluminum foil-lined baking sheet.

Broil 5 inches from heat about 5 minutes on each side or until blistered.

Place peppers in a zip-top plastic bag; seal and let stand 10 minutes to loosen skins. Peel peppers; remove and discard seeds.

Process peppers and remaining ingredients in a food processor until smooth, stopping to scrape down sides. Store pesto in refrigerator up to 1 week.

Note: Poblano peppers are dark green, tapered chili peppers, about 3 inches wide and 4 to 5 inches long. You can find them in the produce section of your grocery store.

7 Layer Mexican Dip

CATHY HUGGINS
SPURS AND FEATHERS

1 cup fat-free sour cream
2 tbsp. reduced-sodium taco seasoning
9 oz. fat-free bean dip, about 1 heaping cup
6 oz. guacamole, about ¾ cup
¼ cup low-fat shredded cheddar cheese
4 medium scallions, chopped
1 small tomato, chopped
6 medium olives, black, sliced or chopped

Combine sour cream and taco seasoning; mix well. Spread bean dip on bottom of a 12-inch round glass serving bowl or edged platter. Top with guacamole, sour cream, cheese, scallions tomatoes and olives.
About ¼ cup dip per serving

SALADS

24-Hour Slaw ~ R. J. Moore

Macaroni Salad ~ Emily White

Mexican Tossed Salad ~ Edith & Art Baker

Romaine Strawberry Almond Salad ~ Lynn & David Odom

Shoe peg Corn Salad ~ Susan & John Moore

Mock Chicken Salad Spread ~ Kay & Eddie Floyd

Shrimp Salad ~ Dona Fowler

Crab Meat Salad ~ Liz & Jimmy Duncan

Hot Chicken Salad ~ Liz & Jimmy Duncan

Antipasto Salad ~ Marjorie & Dom Fusci

B. G.'s Chicken Salad ~ B. G. King

Pasta Salad ~ Cissy & Todd Ellis

Almond Chicken Salad ~ Gwen Adam

Black-eyed pea Salad ~ Orral Anne & Jim Moss

Potato Bacon & Chives Salad ~ Cathy & Gerald Sease

Broccoli Salad ~ Lou Prezioso

Strawberry Salad ~ Thea & Walter Biskow

Shredded Vegetable Slaw ~ Thea & Walter Biskow

Pasta Salad ~ Michele Raeuber

Creamy Ranch Pasta Salad ~ Lisa & Shawn Bishop

Asian Slaw ~ John Frierson

Blueberry Salad ~ Thea & Walter Biskow

Herbed Tomatoes ~ Julie Saunders & Debbie Davis

Noodle Salad ~ Terry Kratofil

Seven Layer Salad ~ Ginger Catoe

Carolina-Clemson game. On the way to the funeral he stopped at a liquor store and called a friend in Columbia who put the radio next to the telephone and R. J. listened to the final moment of the game. Carolina won 13 to 9.

24-Hour Slaw

R. J. MOORE
COURTESY OF JUDY JONES

3 or more lbs. cabbage, shredded
1 large bell pepper cut in small pieces
1 medium jar pimento, chopped

SAUCE
2 cups water
2 cups sugar
2 cups vinegar
2 tablespoon mustard seed
1 tablespoon salt

R.J. MOORE

There is absolutely no question about who is the number one Carolina football fan. That honor would, of course, go to R. J. Moore.

The walls of his Phillip 66 station are covered with photographs of USC athletes. R. J. was once shot while wrestling a gun away from would-be robber. He wounded the robber and both ended up in the hospital. R. J. has survived a stroke and cancer and the loss of his wife. Never-the-less, over a period of more than 30 years, he has missed only one South Carolina football game—home or away.

That was in 1979 when his mother-in law passed away in Arkansas the day before the South

Heat sauce just before it boils (do not boil).

Pour over vegetables and add enough turmeric to color. Let set 24 hours before serving. Will keep in refrigerator 6 to 8 weeks.

Good served with vegetables and meat. Good with hotdogs.

EMILY WHITE

Coaches come and coaches go, as do Athletic Directors at the University of South Carolina. The only thing that remains stable in our Athletic Department is Emily White.

Emily was hired by Paul Dietzel in January of 1967. Since her hiring, seven coaches and eight Athletic Directors have come and gone. In 1988 she had four bosses in one year. Johnny Gregory (interim), Dick Bestwick, Bob Marcum, and King Dixon. She is the one constant and there is a very good reason. She is irreplaceable. Smart and good looking, even tempered and organized she is…well…irreplaceable. I don't know what I'd do without her.

Macaroni Salad

EMILY WHITE
ADMINISTRATIVE ASSISTANT
TO ATHLETIC DIRECTOR MIKE MCGEE

1 box (8 oz.) macaroni
2 hard boiled eggs

1 small jar diced pimento
1 large bell pepper
3 tablespoons salad pickles
1 teaspoon mustard
Mayonnaise
Paprika

After cooking macaroni, drain well. While still warm, add chopped hard boiled eggs, pimento, chopped bell pepper, salad pickles, and mustard. Stir in desired amount of mayonnaise. Sprinkle top with paprika.

This salad is best when made the day before the game and refrigerated overnight.

Cubed ham or chicken may be added to salad, if desired.

Mexican Tossed Salad

EDITH & ART BAKER

Lettuce
1 can pinto beans
Cheese, grated
Onion, dried
Fritos
Catalina dressing

Break lettuce into bite size pieces. Add tomatoes, chilled beans (I don't drain mine), cheese and onion. Add crushed (slightly) Fritos and dressing just before serving.

Cook and stir almonds and sugar in skillet over low heat until sugar is melted and nuts coated and browned. Cool and set aside.

Combine both lettuces, celery, and onions. Refrigerate covered.

When ready to serve, pour dressing over lettuce mixture and add strawberries. Sprinkle nuts over top just before serving.

Shoepeg Corn Salad

SUSAN & JOHN MOORE

16 oz. can shoepeg corn
16 oz. can French style green beans
16 oz. can small green peas
2 oz. jar chopped pimento
1 cup celery, chopped
1 cup green pepper, finely chopped
½ cup onion, chopped
¾ cup sugar
¼ cup salad oil
½ cup vinegar

Drain canned vegetables. Mix vegetables with the fresh vegetables in a 2 quart bowl with a lid that seals tightly. To prepare dressing, heat sugar, oil, and vinegar together in pan on stove. Cool dressing mixture and pour over vegetables. Refrigerate overnight to allow flavors to fully mix.

This salad keeps for may days in the fridge and improves with age. Delicious, easy, and will not easily spoil.

Servings: 12½ cup servings

Romaine Strawberry Almond Salad

LYNN & DAVID ODOM
DAVID ODOM IS HEAD BASKETBALL COACH

DRESSING
½ cup oil
2 tablespoons sugar
2 tablespoons parsley
1 teaspoons salt
4 tablespoons vinegar
Dash of pepper

Combine all ingredients and shake. Chill at least one hour.

SALAD
¼ cup sliced almonds
1½ tablespoon sugar
½ head leaf lettuce, torn
½ cup chopped celery
4 green onions, sliced
2 cups sliced strawberries

Mock Chicken Salad

KAY B. FLOYD

1 cup pecans, chopped fine
1 hard boiled egg, chopped fine
1 small bottle of olives, drained and chopped fine
1 small onion, grated
1 pint mayonnaise

Mix first four ingredients well then blend in mayonnaise. Refrigerate. Keeps well. Makes enough spread for one loaf of bread.

Shrimp Salad

DONA W. FOWLER

3 hard boiled eggs, chopped
½ cup Hellmann's mayonnaise
1 tablespoon fresh lemon juice
½ teaspoon salt
1½ teaspoons ground black pepper
1 cup celery, chopped
1 tablespoons Durkee's Sauce
1 tablespoon capers
2 lbs. boiled, deveined shrimp
(If using large shrimp, (30-35 count) cut in several
   pieces)

Mix mayonnaise; lemon juice; eggs; salt; pepper; celery; Durkee's Sauce and capers. Toss shrimp in last. Cover and refrigerate.

JIMMY DUNCAN

Jimmy was a teammate of mine and he was well-tough. The kind of guy you want to play with, not against.

His first job after college was with Commercial Credit in Charlotte. His boss told him when he hired him; "I'm sending you to Rockingham, North Carolina, and there are only two things that can happen to you in Rockingham; you can quit or get fired."

Jim's job was to repossess lumber trucks. Can you imagine foreclosing on angry, delinquent, mountain lumber jacks? He lasted 11 months until one such angry driver turned a bear loose on him. I said he was tough but not stupid, so he moved on.

He spent 22 years with, first Campbell Soups and Reynolds Aluminum.

He returned to Charlotte in 1983 as Executive Vice President of Marketing with the Charlotte Motor Speedway.

Crab Meat Salad

LIZ & JIMMY DUNCAN

FROM FROSSIE JOHNSON'S "FLOSSIE'S FAVORITES"

½ lb. shrimp
Onions, chopped fine
Mayonnaise
1 lb. crabmeat
Celery, chopped fine
Cavendar's Greek seasoning to taste

Mix all ingredients and chill.

Hot Chicken Salad

LIZ & JIMMY DUNCAN

FROM FROSSIE JOHNSON'S "FLOSSIE'S FAVORITES"

2 cups diced, cooked chicken
½ cup silvered almonds, toasted
1 tablespoon grated lemon rind
½ teaspoon pepper
1½ cups crushed potato chips
1½ cups diced celery
2 hard-cooked eggs, chopped
1 cup mayonnaise
2 teaspoons lemon juice
1½ cups (6 oz.) shredded Cheddar cheese

Combine chicken, celery, almonds, eggs, onion, mayonnaise, lemon rind, lemon juice, and pepper in a large bowl. Mix well. Spoon chicken mixture into a lightly greased shallow 2 qt. casserole. Sprinkle with cheese and top with potato chips.

Bake at 375 degrees for 25 minutes.

DOM FUSCI

Dom was a three letter man at Carolina in 1942, 1943 and 1946. He served in the Pacific (1944-45) in World War 11. He is in the State's Hall of Fame and has the best memory of any 100 year old man I know.

Antipasta Salad

MARJORIE & DOMINIC FUSCI

1½ tbsp. red wine vinegar
3 tbsp. olive oil
1 clove garlic, minced
1 tsp. Italian seasoning
¼ tsp. salt
8 oz. Mozzarella, diced
1 can artichoke hearts, quartered
1 small bulb fennel, thinly sliced
1 small can black olives, sliced
1 tbsp. lemon juice
4 oz. salami, thinly sliced

4 oz. prosciutto, thinly sliced
3 tbs. red Italian peppers
1 small Romaine lettuce, washed and chopped

To make dressing: Whisk together red wine vinegar, olive oil, garlic, lemon juice, Italian seasoning, and salt.

Combine Mozzarella, artichoke hearts, black olives fennel, salami and Prosciutto in small bowl. Toss with 2½ tablespoons dressing. Set aside.

Toss chopped Romaine with remaining dressing. Place in serving bowl or platter. Pour cheese mixture on top. Garnish with chopped peppers.

B.G.'s Chicken Salad

B. G. KING

1 package chicken breast
4 eggs
½ jar sweet cube pickles
2 to 3 tablespoons mayonnaise
2 tablespoons sugar
Salt and pepper to taste

Boil chicken, cut into chunks. Boil eggs, mash. Combine all dry ingredients. Sprinkle sugar, salt, pepper;
Add pickle and mayonnaise.

Put on bread of choice, but best results use Sourdough Bread.

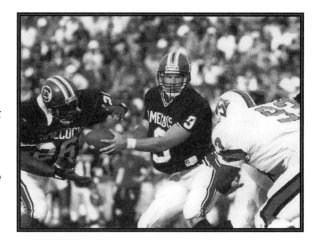

TODD ELLIS

A four year starter. Todd threw for a school record 9,954 yards from 1986-1989. His 97 yard toss to Robert Brooks was a school record until last years 99-yarder from Pinkins to Troy Williamson. His 77 yard non scoring pass to Ryan Bethea is also a school record. Todd threw for 425 yards in on game and is second only to Steve Tanneyhill. Todd is in his second year of doing play by play on the Gamecock network.

Pasta Salad

CISSY & TODD ELLIS

1 box bow tie pasta
1 cucumber
1 tomato
1 medium purple onion
1 container of feta cheese
1 bottle of Giards Romano Cheese Dressing

CONTINUED

Boil pasta. Chop tomato, cucumber and onion. Mix all together with feta cheese. Pour bottle of dressing on top and mix-or wait to pour dressing if not eating right away. Great with any kind of crackers

Make three days ahead. Rinse and drain peas, add onion, green pepper, and pimento. Mix other 6 ingredients together. Mix and pour over peas. Refrigerate for 3 days if possible. Canned peas can be used.

Almond Chicken Salad
GWEN ADAMS

1 lb. cooked chicken, diced
1 cup mayonnaise
1 cup sour cream
¼ cup almonds toasted (sliced) 350 for 10 min.
2 tablespoons onions, chopped
1 tablespoons dried tarragon
½ teaspoon salt
⅛ teaspoon white pepper

Mix all ingredients. Refrigerate

Potato Salad—Bacon & Chives
CATHY & GERALD SEASE

6 cups quartered, unpeeled red potatoes
¾ cup mayonnaise
2 tablespoons stone ground mustard or Dijon
8 slices bacon cooked crisp
¼ cup chopped chives or green onions

Add potatoes to boiling water; cook 15 minutes or until tender; drain. Mix mayonnaise and mustard in large bowl. Add potatoes, bacon and chives; mix lightly and refrigerate.

Black-Eyed Pea Salad
ORRAL ANNE & JIM MOSS

4 cups cooked dried black eyed peas, drained
1 cup salad oil
¼ cup vinegar (cider or wine)
½ teaspoon garlic powder
1 teaspoon salt
1 dash of Tabasco
Freshly ground black pepper
1 small green pepper, sliced thin
1 medium onion, sliced thin
1 jar pimento

Broccoli Salad
LOU PREZIOSO

2 10 oz. packages of broccoli spears
1 7 oz. jar stuffed olives, chopped
3 hard boiled eggs, chopped
½ cup onion, chopped
1 cup celery, chopped
1 cup Hellmann's mayonnaise

Undercook broccoli. Drain and let cool. Chop into 1-inch cubes. Mix with remaining ingredients. Chill.

Strawberry Salad

THETA & WALTER BRISKOW

1 6 oz. box wild strawberry jello
1 small can crushed pineapple
2 cups boiling water
1 10 oz. package frozen sliced strawberries
1 cup chopped pecans

Drain strawberries and pineapple and reserve the juices. Dissolve the jello in the boiling water and add fruit juices. Add all other ingredients and pour into a 2 qt. Pyrex dish. Chill until firm. Spread topping on firm salad.

TOPPING
4 oz. cream cheese, softened
1 teaspoon vanilla
1 cup sour cream
⅓ cup sugar

Whip cream cheese and sugar until blended. Fold in vanilla and sour cream.
Servings: 8

Shredded Vegetable Slaw

THETA & WALTER BRISKOW
FROM HER COOKBOOK

1 small bunch fresh broccoli
2 medium carrots, peeled
1 purple onion
1 bottle Old Dutch dressing
1 small head cauliflower
1 small bell pepper
½ small head purple cabbage
1 teaspoon each salt and coarse black pepper

Fit the shred blade on the food processor and shred all vegetables. Put in large covered bowl and sprinkle with salt and pepper. Stir well and pour dressing over vegetables. Cover and refrigerate overnight. Drain well before serving. Save the dressing to put any left-overs back in it.
Servings: 10 to 12

Pasta Salad

MICHELE RACUBER

2 medium carrots, diced
8 ounces elbow macaroni, cooked, Rinse in cold water & drain well. Do not overcook the pasta.
1 large green pepper, diced
1 medium onion, diced
2 stalks celery, diced
1 cucumber, peeled and diced
1 large tomato, diced
Toss the above ingredients leaving the tomato to last

MARINADE
½ cup salad oil
½ cup apple cider vinegar or regular cider
¼ cup sugar
Salt and pepper to taste

Combine all the ingredients, mix well, pour over the pasta salad, mix well.
  Let stand several hours or overnight.

Ranch Pasta Salad
LISA & SHAWN BISHOP

2 packages Betty Crocker Suddenly Salad Ranch and Bacon Pasta Salad Mix
1 cup mayonnaise
2 tablespoons Dijon Mustard
2 medium stalks celery, thinly sliced
6 hard cooked eggs, coarsely chopped
1 hard cooked egg, sliced
Paprika

Boil both Past-vegetable pouches uncovered 15 minutes until tender. Drain pasta. Rinse with cold water. Shake to drain well. Stir together seasoning mixes, mayonnaise, mustard and celery. Stir in pasta and chopped eggs.

Garnish with hard cooked egg slices and paprika

Asian Slaw
JOHN FRIERSON

1½ pks beef Ramin Noodles
2 (8 ½ oz.) slaw mix (Dole)
1 cup sliced almonds toasted
1 oz. sunflower seed
1 bunch green onions chopped
¾ cup vegetable oil
⅓ cup white vineger
½ cup sugan
Use two packets with noodles in dressing

Crunch noodles and place in bottom of large bowl. Top with slaw mix, sprinkle with nuts and onions. Wisk together beef flavor packets with oil, sugar, and vineger. Pour over layers in bowl.Cover and chill 24 hours. Toss before serving. Will keep one week.

Blueberry Salad
THETA & WALTER BRISKOW

1 6 oz. box black cherry jello
1 can blueberry pie filling
2 cups boiling water
1 20 oz. can crushed pineapple

Put jello in boiling water and stir until completely dissolved. Add pie filling and drained pineapple. Pour into a 2 qt. Pyrex dish and chill until firm.
Servings: 8

Herbed Tomatoes
JULIE SANDERS & DEBBIE DAVIS

4 firm ripe tomatoes
Dash salt and pepper
2 tablespoons minced green onion
4 tablespoons parsley, minced
½ teaspoon dried oregano leaves
1 cup fresh bread crumbs
1 large clove garlic, pressed
2 tablespoon olive oil

Cut tomatoes in half. Squeeze out juice and seeds. Sprinkle with salt. Drain Combine green onions, parsley, oregano, bread crumbs and garlic. Place tomatoes in oiled baking dish. Fill with crumb mixture. Drizzle with oil.

Bake at 400 degrees for 15 minutes until crumbs have browned and tomatoes are soft.
Serves: 4

Noodle Salad
TERRY KRATOFIL

1 lb. box elbow noodles
½ small onlon-chopped flne
2 or 3 celery stalk-cut fine
1 small green pepper-chopped fine
1 to ½ cups sliced green stuffed olives (with red centers)-drained
¾ lb. piece about 1" thick Virginia Ham from deli (my mother-in-law used canned Treet which I like better than the ham, but when people say how good this is and ask what meat it is they seem to freak out when you say it is Treet for some reason),diced into small pieces
1 cup mayonnaise
Salt and pepper to taste

Cook noodles according to package, drain, rinse and cool. Chop onion, celery, green pepper and ham and place in a large bowl.

Add cooked noodles to bowl. Add green Spanish sliced olives. Add mayonnaise and mix together. Add salt to taste. If you like more mayonnaise, add it.

Cool for a few hours and serve

Seven Layer Salad

GINGER CATOE

1 head of lettuce, torn into bite sized pieces
1 medium onion, diced
1 10 ounce box frozen peas
4 eggs, boiled and chopped
8 slices bacon, fried and crumbled
Mild cheddar cheese, shredded
2 cups of Mayonnaise or Miracle Whip
2 tablespoon sugar

In a large see-though glass bowl, place one layer of each in this order: Lettuce, onion, frozen peas, and eggs. Mix together mayonnaise and sugar and spread over eggs. Sprinkle cheese and then bacon on top. Alternate layers. Refrigerate overnight. You can also use some of the following as layers: sliced radishes, chopped cucumber, sliced fresh mushrooms, chopped green peppers, or tomatoes.
Servings: 8 to 10

SANDWICHES

Billy Thomas' Ham Sandwiches ~ Al Johnson

Shrimp Salad Sandwich ~ Jim & Orral Anne Moss

Carrot Sandwich ~ Jim & Orral Anne Moss

Spinach Sandwich ~ Jim & Orral Anne Moss

Eggplant, Tomato, Goat cheese Grilled Sandwich ~ Gerald & Cathy Sease

Football Player's Hot Dog ~ Kathi & Jimmy Mithchell

Cocky's Meat Loaf Sandwich ~ Kathi & Jimmy Mitchell

Baked Virginia Ham ~ Kathi & Jimmy Mitchell

Mary Ann's Pimento Cheese ~ Courtesy of Durry & Debbie Faulk

Pimiento Cheese ~ Zoe & Alex Sanders

Western Barbecue Super Subs ~ Lisa & Shawn Bishop

Sandwich Wraps ~ Lisa & Shawn Bishop

Mrs. Tucker's Shrimp Salad Sanwiches
ORRAL ANNE & JIM MOSS

2 lbs. fresh medium shrimp
1 cup celery, chopped
½ lemon, juice
6 boiled eggs, chopped
Mayonnaise, enough to mix
Salt and pepper to taste

Boil shrimp to pink stage, drain and chop. Add the rest of the ingredients and mix. Use Pepperidge Farm bread so sandwiches won't be soggy. Store in ice chest.

Billy Thomas' Ham Sandwiches
AL JOHNSON

2 oz. package Bryans Honey Baked Ham
Hellmans Mayonnaise
Claussen White Bread
Pepper

Spread mayonnaise on bread. Place 2 slices of ham on a piece of bread and pepper. Top with another piece of bread and cut into triangles. Place in plastic container and refrigerate overnight. Never have any to take home after a ballgame.

Carrot Sandwiches
ORRAL ANNE & JIM MOSS

3 oz. cream cheese
1 cup carrots, grated
1 small onion, grated
½ teaspoon Worcestershire
½ cup nuts, grated

Mix well and use Pepperidge Farm Bread

Spinach Sandwiches
ORRAL ANNE & JIM MOSS

2 boxes frozen shopped spinach (reg. size)
¾ cups onions, chopped
¾ cups sour cream
½ cups mayonnaise

Mix well and refrigerate about 1 hour. Spread on Pepperidge Farm Bread

Eggplant, Tomato, Goat Cheese
CATHY & GERALD SEASE

3 tablespoons olive oil
2 large cloves garlic
1 12" baguette cut horizontally
1 small eggplant cut lengthwise into 6½" slices
3 medium tomatoes cut into 10 slices, total
3 oz. soft goat cheese (Montrachet)
12 fresh basil leaves

Prepare Barbeque at medium high heat. Combine oil and garlic in small bowl. Let stand 5 minutes.

Brush cut sides of baguette and both sides of eggplant slices and tomato slices with garlic oil. Grill cut sides of baguette until toasted; about 2 minutes. Transfer baguette, cut side up, to plate. Season eggplant and tomatoes with salt and pepper. Grill eggplant until cooked through about 6 minutes per side; transfer to plate. Grill tomatoes until warmed though, about 1 minute per side; transfer to plate.

Spread goat cheese on bread, dividing equally. Overlap eggplant slices, then tomato slices on

baguette halves, covering completely. Garnish with fresh basil leaves. Cut each sandwich diagonally into 4 sections, and serve.

For tailgating, place bacon press or heavy fry pan on finished sandwiches to compress.

JIMMY MITCHELL

Jimmy was one of USC's all time best receivers. He was an All ACC selection in 1970 and was the Gamecocks leading receiver in 1970 and 1971 with 88 catches for 1,460 yards.

Football Player's Hot Dogs
KATHI & JIMMY MITCHELL

2 tablespoons onions, minced
2 12oz. cans of beer
2 tablespoons Worcestershire sauce
½ cup chili sauce
24 all beef hot dogs, halved
12 French rolls, split

CONTINUED

In a sauce pot mix onion, beer, Worcestershire sauce, chili sauce and hot dogs together. Simmer for 30 minutes. Serve on split rolls.
Servings: 12

Cocky's Meat Loaf Sandwiches
KATHI & JIMMY MITCHELL

3 cups onions, chopped (2 Lg. onions)
2 tablespoons olive oil
2 teaspoons kosher salt
1 teaspoon pepper
1 teaspoon fresh thyme leaves (½ teaspoon dried)
⅓ cup chicken broth
1½ teaspoon tomato paste
5 lbs. ground sirloin
1½ cups plain dry bread crumbs
3 large eggs, beaten
¾ cup ketchup

Preheat the oven to 325 degrees. In a medium sauté pan cook the onions, olive oil, salt, pepper and thyme until the onions are transparent, abou5t 15 minutes. Add the Worcestershire sauce, chicken stock, and tomato paste and mix well. Allow to cool to room temperature.

Combine the ground sirloin, bread crumbs, eggs, and onion mixture in a large bowl. Mix well and shape into a log on baking sheet. Spread the ketchup evenly on top. Bake for 1¼ hours until cooked.

Serve hot, room temp. or cold in a sandwich (assorted breads and rolls).

Baked Virginia Ham
KATHI & JIMMY MITCHELL

1 8-10 lb. fully cooked smoked ham
3 garlic cloves
8½ oz. mango chutney
½ cup Dijon mustard
1 cup light brown sugar, packed
Zest of 1 orange
¼ cup orange juice

Preheat oven to 350 degrees. Place the ham in a heavy roasting pan. Mince the garlic in a food processor. Add the chutney, mustard, brown sugar, orange zest and orange juice and process until smooth. Pour the glaze over the ham and bake for 1 hour until the ham is fully heated and the glaze is well browned.

Serve at room temp. with assorted breads or mini muffins.

Mary Ann's Pimento Cheese
DURRY & DEBBIE FAULK

8 oz. Extra sharp cheese
8 oz. Medium cheese
8 oz. Pepperjack cheese
7 oz. Pimento, chopped
1 cup mayonnaise
Salt, pepper, garlic powder & cayenne pepper to taste
Add few tablespoons of evaporated milk or half and half to make creamier

Mix and enjoy on sandwiches, burgers, celery, crackers or whatever your choose.

Pimento Cheese
ZOE & ALEX SANDERS

1 lb. extra sharp cheddar cheese
8 oz. chopped pimiento, drained
¼ cup Hellmann's mayonnaise
¼ teaspoon salt
½ teaspoon pepper

Grate cheese on large side of grater or with grating blade of food processor. Combine cheese, pimiento, mayonnaise, salt and pepper. Mix gently with large spoon to preserve the texture of cheese and pimientos.

To make pimiento cheese sandwiches, spread each sandwich with 5 tablespoons pimiento cheese.

For party servings, cut crusts off and quarter.
Servings: 7 sandwiches or 24 party quarters

Sandwich Wraps
LISA & SHAWN BISHOP

1 cup Blue Cheese Salad Dressing
8 8 to 10-inch whole wheat or Southwest flavor
   flour tortillas
8 Romaine lettuce leaves
8 slices bacon, crisp cooked
4 Roma tomatoes, seeded and cut into thin wedges
1 cup shredded Mozzarella cheese
Rotisserie chicken, shredded

Spread salad dressing on one side of each tortilla. Top with lettuce, bacon, tomato, cheese and chicken. Tightly roll up each tortilla. Wrap each tortilla in plastic wrap and chill 2 to 4 hours.

Western Barbecue Duper Subs
LISA & SHAWN BISHOP

½ cup guacamole
3 cups shredded Rotisserie chicken
¼ cup barbecue sauce
1 small green pepper, thinly sliced
6 soft Hoagie Rolls, split

Spread guacamole on cut sides of rolls. Layer with chicken. Drizzle with barbecue sauce. Add green pepper.

VEGGIES & CASSEROLES

Chicken Pie ~ **Pat & Humpy Wheeler**

Breakfast Casserole ~ **Susie & Heyward King**

Pizza Casserole ~ **Jan & Alvin Roof**

Oyster Pie Casserole ~ **Billy Canada**

Red Beans and Rice ~ **Billy Canada**

Hash Brown Potatoes Casserole ~ **Kim & Jay Frye**

Twice Baked potato ~ **Steve Tanneyhill /Bright Stevenson**

Grilled Vegetable ~ **Cathy & Gerald Sease**

Summer Tomato Pie ~ **Zoe and Alex Sanders**

Winter Tomato Pie ~ **Zoe and Alex Sanders**

Twice Baked Potatoes ~ **Sherrill R. Bland**

Mary Ann's Potato Salad ~ **Courtesy of Debbie Faulk**

Baked Potato Casserole Puff ~ **Ryan Brewer**

Bean Burritos ~ **Jean & Jim Pool**

Corn Pudding ~ **Rae & Edwin Floyd**

Gan's Baked Beans ~ **Melisson Murdaugh**

English Pea Casserole ~ **Sterling Sharpe**

Macaroni Pie ~ **Rita & Charles Ray Brown**

Nana's Macaroni & Cheese ~ **Caitlyn Murdaugh**

Oyster Pie ~ **Hannali & Red Furguson**

Onion Rings ~ **J.R. Wilburn**

Potato Casserole ~ **Terry Kratofil**

Breakfast Casserole ~ **Kathy Fulmer**

H.A. "HUMPY" WHEELER

Probably a better boxer than a football player, Humpy lettered in both sports at Carolina. He compiled a record of 40-2 in Golden Glove competition and is a member of the Carolina Boxing Hall of Fame.

In the spring of 1961 I asked Humpy what he was going to do when he graduated. He told me he was going back to Charlotte and get involved in racing. I advised him that that would be a mistake. "Racing is a redneck sport that is going nowhere."

Humpy discarded my advice, and went back to Charlotte to work as a sportswriter, television director, real estate manager and a dirt track promoter.

He became president and G.M. of what was then the Charlotte Motor Speedway in 1975.

I lost track of Humpy for a few years, but in 1984 I was sitting in a bar in Columbia, S.C. when someone made mention that Humpy was going to build 40 condominium units that overlooked the racetrack.

Never without an opinion, I got on the phone to warn him against it. Have you lost your mind, I demanded? Who do you think is going to buy a condo overlooking a race track?"

Corporate America, he answered calmly. I was only going to build 30, but I've already sold 40 and the architectural plans haven't been drawn up yet.

In the past ten years what is now, Lowe's Motor Speedway, has increased its seating capacity from 75,000 seats to 167,000 and is the first super speedway to host night racing.

In 1995 they went public to become the first publicly traded motor sports company on the New York Stock Exchange.

Humpy has never asked me for advise, but had he, I would have advised him against all of the above.

Melt in Your Mouth Chicken Pie

PAT & HUMPY WHEELER

1 4-5 to 6 lb. chicken, cooked, boned and shredded
1½ to 2 cups of reserved broth from chicken
1 10 3¾ oz. cream of chicken soup
1 stick butter, melted
1 cup self rising flour
½ teaspoon salt
Dash of pepper
1 cup buttermilk

Place chicken in a greased 9 x 13 inch baking dish. In a saucepan combine soup and broth and when blended, pour over chicken.

Combine flour, butter, salt and pepper and buttermilk. Spoon over top of chicken and broth. Bake at 425 degrees. Cook 25 30 minutes. Servings: 6 to 8

Breakfast Casserole

SUSIE & HEYWARD KING

1 lb. hot bulk pork sausage
2 cups milk
1 teaspoon dry mustard
½ teaspoon salt
6 eggs, beaten
2 slices bread, torn into crumbs
1 cup sharp cheddar cheese, grated

Brown sausage; drain well. Beat eggs, salt, milk and dry mustard together. Layer bread crumbs, sausage and cheese in an 8 x 12 Pyrex dish. Pour egg mixture over top. Cover and refrigerate over night. Bake at 350 degrees for 45 minutes.

Pizza Casserole

JAN & ALVIN ROOF

1 lb. hamburger meat
1 onion, chopped
Salt, pepper, garlic powder and Italian seasoning, to taste
Rotini Twist Noodles
3 small cans of tomato sauce
Pepperoni
Sliced sharp cheese
Sliced mushrooms

In frying pan, brown hamburger and add a chopped onion. Season to taste with salt, pepper, garlic powder and Italian seasoning. Cook Rotini Twist Noodles about 3/4 of a 16 oz. box. Drain in large baking dish, layer meat, twist noodles, 3 small cans of tomato sauce, and then sliced pepperoni, then sliced sharp cheese and 1 can drained sliced mushrooms. Bake at 350 until it bubbles and cheese melts. Approx. 45 minutes

Oyster Pie

BILLY CANADA

1 quart fresh oysters
12 saltines, crumbled
4 eggs, beaten
¼ cup cream
⅛ lb. butter, melted
Black pepper, to taste

Mix together in casserole and bake at 350 degrees. Preheated oven for 30 minutes.

Red Beans and Rice

BILLY CANADA

2 lbs. dried beans
1 ham bone
2 large onions, chopped
2 cloves garlic, chopped
Cayenne pepper, salt & pepper to taste

Wash beans, cover in cold water overnight. Using the same water, cook over medium heat. Add onions, garlic, ham bone, pepper and salt. Hold enough water to cover. Bring to a boil. Turn heat to low. Cover and cook 3-8 hours. Serve over rice and with corn bread.

Hash Brown Casserole

KIM & JAY FRYE

4 cups frozen shredded hash browns
1 can potato soup
8 oz. sour cream
8 oz. cheddar cheese
½ cup chopped onion
Salt and pepper to taste

Save half of cheese. Combine all other ingredients and bake at 350 degrees for 1 hour covered in a buttered baking dish (2 qt.). Uncover and sprinkle with remaining cheese until melted.
Servings: 8

Twice Baked Potatoes

STEVE TANNEYHILL
COURTESY OF BRIGHT STEVENSON

Potatoes (count one for two peoples)
Onion, chopped very fine
Milk and butter, just a little
Sour cream
Sharp cheddar cheese, grated

Bake potatoes until done. Cut in half length wise. Take meat out of the potato skins and mix with a little butter and milk. Add onions and sour cream. Salt and pepper, to taste. Put potato mixture back into the skins. Top with cheese. In a 400 degrees oven bake until cheese is melted. Then it is ready.

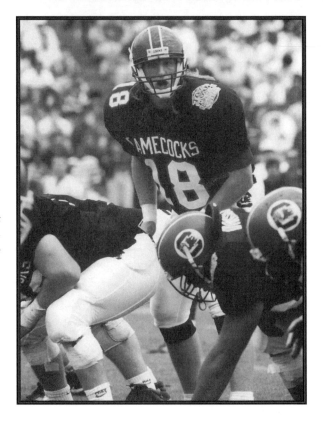

STEVE TANNEYHILL

Steve holds many school records including; net yards gained in a single game (512) passes attempted in one game (58), consecutive completions (18) passing yardage in one games (473), passes completed in one game he is 1st, 2nd, 3rd, and 4th. His 3,094 passing yards in one season is second to Todd Ellis.

No one seems to know where Steve is today, but that's not surprising. We gave Steve Bright Stevenson's Twice Baked Potato recipe, because I've always thought both of them were only Half Baked.

Twice Baked Potatoes

STEVE TANNEYHILL
COURTESY OF BRIGHT STEVENSON

Potatoes (count one for two peoples)
Onion, chopped very fine
Milk and butter, just a little
Sour cream
Sharp cheddar cheese, grated

Bake potatoes until done. Cut in half length wise. Take meat out of the potato skins and mix with a little butter and milk. Add onions and sour cream. Salt and pepper, to taste. Put potato mixture back into the skins. Top with cheese. In a 400 degrees oven bake until cheese is melted. Then it is ready.

Grilled Vegetables

CATHY & GEORGE SEASE

2 red bell peppers
2 yellow bell peppers
1 small eggplant cut in half lengthwise, approx. 1 lb.
16 asparagus spears, about 1 lb.
1 medium zucchini or
Squash, cut in half lengthwise
8 Italian plum tomatoes
2 tablespoons olive oil
½ teaspoon pepper
¼ teaspoon salt
Ranch salad dressing
Parmesan cheese, optional

Brush first 6 ingredients with oil; sprinkle evenly with black pepper and salt. Place bell peppers on grill rack coated with cooking spray; grill 5 minutes. Add eggplant; grill 5 minutes; add asparagus; grill 5 minutes. Add zucchini and grill 5 minutes. Add tomatoes and grill 5 minutes or until all vegetables are tender, turning as needed. Remove from grill.

Cut each bell pepper into quarters; eggplant half's and zucchini halves into 4 equal pieces.

Serve with Ranch Dressing. Serving size is 2 quarters each, 1 eggplant, 2 asparagus, 1 zucchini, and 1 tomato. If not serving with Ranch dressing, sprinkle with parmesan cheese. For tailgating, don't forget the toothpicks!

Summer Tomato Pie

ZOE & ALEX SANDERS

2 prebaked 9 inch Easy pie crusts
1½ pounds ripe tomatoes
½ teaspoon salt
1 teaspoon black pepper
6 tablespoons fresh basil, chopped or 2 Tbl. dried
1 cup jumbo yellow onion, chopped
3 cups (12 oz.) extra sharp cheddar cheese, grated
1 cup of Hellmann's mayonnaise

Dip tomatoes in boiling water for 1 minute and peel. Slice ½-inch thick. Drain dry on paper towel.

Divide ingredients evenly between the two pies and follows: Cover bottom of crusts with tomatoes. Sprinkle with salt; pepper and mayonnaise. Cover pies loosely, but completely, spreading mayonnaise mixture with fingers. Do not press this mix.

When baked, the light and fluffy mayonnaise and

CONTINUED

cheese mixture will be similar in texture to a quiche.

Bake pies at 350 degrees for 30 to 35 minutes, or until cheese is bubbly and beginning to brown. Remove from oven and let set 20 to 30 minutes before slicing.
Servings: 8

Winter Tomato Pie
ZOE & ALEX SANDERS
FROM HER BOOK
"ENTERTAINING AT COLLEGE OF CHARLESTON"

There are several months when tomatoes have very poor texture and no taste. Canned tomatoes are inexpensive and make a good pie. We use Certo tomatoes.

2 prebaked 9 inch Easy pie crusts
2 (28 oz.) cans whole tomatoes, drained, chopped, and juice pressed out
½ teaspoon salt
1 teaspoon black pepper
2 tablespoons dried basil
1 cup jumbo yellow onion, chopped
1 cup of Hellman's mayonnaise
3 cups (12 oz.) extra sharp cheddar cheese, grated

Instructions for making Winter Tomato Pie are the same as Summer Tomato Pie.

Twice Baked Potatoes
SHERRILL BLAND

4 to 6 large baking potatoes
1 16 oz. container sour cream
Salt & pepper
Chives
2 cups grated cheddar cheese

Bake potatoes until done (best way we've found is to microwave them for 15 minutes then in the oven at 350 degrees until done). This makes the outside skin a little drier and easier to scoop the meat of the potato out. Once potatoes are baked, cut in half, lengthwise, and scoop out the meat of the potato without breaking the skin. Mix the potato, sour cream and salt & pepper to taste, until you have a smooth, thick consistency. Mix in chives and cheddar cheese to your liking. Heap the mix back into the potato skins and top with more cheddar cheese.

When ready to eat, just wrap them in tin foil and throw on the grill with whatever you're cooking to heat them through.

Mary Ann's Potato Salad
COURTESY OF DEBBIE FAULK

5 lb. bag red new potatoes, boiled and peeled
4 hard-boiled eggs
1 cup chopped olives or more to taste
1 2 cup mayonnaise
2 Tbsp. mustard
Salt, pepper, garlic powder & cayenne pepper to taste

Allow potatoes to cool some. Add additional ingredients, mix gently and enjoy

Baked Potato Casserole Puff

RYAN BREWER

2 cups seasoned mashed potatoes
1 tablespoon pimento, chopped
½ pint cottage cheese
1 teaspoon onion salt
2 eggs, beaten
½ pt. sour cream
1 tablespoon chives

Stir all ingredients together and put into greased casserole. Sprinkle with paprika. Bake one hour at 350 degrees.

Bean Burritos

JEAN & JIM POOLE

1 can of re-fried beans
1 packet of taco seasoning
Jalapeño peppers
½ cup of salsa
Shredded sharp cheddar cheese
10 to 12 flour tortillas

Mix re-fried beans, taco seasoning, salsa and chopped jalapeño peppers (according to taste).

Place about two heaping tablespoons of mixture in tortilla and sprinkle with cheese and roll.

If using large tortillas cut in half.

Serve with extra salsa and peppers on the side.

RYAN BREWER

Mr. Football in the State of Ohio. Ryan was one of Lou Holtz's first recruits at Carolina. A wide receiver, running back, kick off and punt returner.

M.V.P. in the 2001 Out Back Bowl. Ryan rushed for 109 yards, caught three passes for 92 yards and returned two punts for 18 yards and scored all three of South Carolina touchdowns as the Gamecocks upset Ohio State 24-7.

Injuries hampered him in his senior year, but he was an inspiration leader and co-captained the team. He played with his head and his heart and was my favorite player.

Corn Pudding
RAE & EDWIN FLOYD

1 can cream corn
3 eggs, separated
2 tablespoons flour
2 tablespoons sugar
1 teaspoon salt
½ cup butter, melted
½ cup sweet milk

Beat egg yolk. Add corn, flour, sugar, salt, butter and milk. Fold in beaten egg whites. Bake in greased dish in 350 oven for 40 minutes. Preheat oven.

Gan's Baked Beans
MELISSA MURDAUGH

Bacon
3 large cans pork/beans
¼ cup ketchup
½ bag of brown sugar
1 tbsp. Salt
Black pepper
2 medium onions
½ cup sugar

Mix all except bacon. Pour into pan. Tope with bacon. Bake at 350 degrees for 30 to 45 minutes.

STERLING SHARPE

South Carolina's all-time pass receiving leader with 169 career catches for 2,497 yards, 17 touchdowns. Top single season receiver with 74 catches for 1,166 yards, 10 TD's in 1986. His 104 yard kickoff return is the longest in school's history. Two time All American. Was an All Pro Player for seven years with the Green Bay Packers.

English Pea Casserole
STERLING SHARPE

2 large cans peas, drained
1 can cut-up water chestnuts
1 small jar cut-up pimentos
½ cup chopped bell pepper
1 can mushroom soup

1 stick butter
1 cup celery
1 cup chopped onion

Melt butter; add celery, onion and bell pepper. Cook until soft. Add remainder of ingredients; cover with buttered bread crumbs. Bake at 350 degrees until bubbly.

1 cup cooked noodles
1½ cups milk (can use skim milk)
½ teaspoon salt
2 eggs
Pepper to taste
4 tablespoons butter (can use less)

Mix and bake at 350 degrees for 1 hour.

Macaroni Pie

JUDGE RITA BROWN & CHARLES RAY

1½ cups uncooked macaroni noodles
4 eggs
2 cans evaporated milk
1 stick butter
8 12 oz. cup up sharp cheese
4 oz. cut up Velveeta cheese
Salt and pepper to taste

Cook macaroni in salted water until done. Drain. While noodles are hot pour them in mixture of 4 eggs beaten with 2 cans of evaporated milk. Cut up 1 stick of butter and add to mixture. Add cut up cheese and mix well. Sprinkle salt and pepper over mixture. Pour in a 9 x 13 x 2 inch Pyrex dish and bake at 350 degrees for 45 minutes or until mixture is firm.

If need more liquid, you can add some whole milk to mixture and stir well.

Oyster Pie

HANNALI & RED FURGUSON

1 pint oysters
1 stick butter
Oysterettes or crushed Saltines
½ cup milk
Few drops of Worcestershire sauce
2 eggs
Salt and pepper, to taste
Dash of hot sauce

Drain oysters, reserving liquid. Place layer of oysters, top with oysterettes, part of melted butter, repeat second layer. Beat eggs, milk, juice from oysters, sauces, salt and pepper. Pour over and top with oysterettes.

Bale at 400 for 25 to 30 minutes. Double or triple recipe for crowd.

Nana's Macaroni & Cheese

CAITLYN MURDAUGH

1 cup grated cheese

J.R. WILBURN

J.R. was the Gamecock's leading receiver in 1964 and 1965. He was also out standing in track. J.R. was drafted by the Pittsburg Steelers and played there for five seasons.

Onion Rings

J.R. WILBURN
COURTESY OF C.W.

These should be served the moment they come out of the fryer.

2 large onions, fresh Vidalia, or Sweet Texas
1 cup all- purpose flour
2 cups buttermilk
1 tablespoon sugar (I don't use the sugar)
1 teaspoon baking powder
½ teaspoon salt
Peanut oil

Cut onions into ½-inch slices, and separate into rings. Set aside. Whisk together flour and next 4 ingredients until smooth.

Pour oil to a depth of 2 inches into a Dutch oven; heat to 375 degrees.

Dip onion rings in batter, coating well. Fry, a few rings at a time, until golden.

Drain on paper towels. Serve immediately.

Potato Casserole

TERRY KRATOFIL

10 cups hash browns—any brand-it is a large bag
¼ cup + 1 Tablespoons butter or margarine
1 can cream of chicken soup
12 oz. sour cream
½ cup green onions, chopped
2 cups grated cheddar cheese
1 cup corn flakes, crushed

Preheat oven to 375 degrees. Add 5 cups of frozen hash browns. In a separate bowl, mix soup sour cream, milk and green onions. Sprinkle on remaining cheese. Then cover with crushed corn flakes and drizzle 2 tablespoons melted butter on top. Bake for 55 minutes.

I get these ready the night before. Put in the refrigerator. Cook them while I get other things ready for tailgating the next morning.

Ultimate Tailgater Breakfast Casserole

KATHY FULMER

1 lb. sausage, hot or mild
3 tablespoons margarine
2 small cans mild green chilies, chopped
1½ cups sour cream
4 cups shredded cheddar cheese
4 English muffins
12 eggs beaten

Brown sausage until crumbly, drain. Split English Muffins. Butter inside with 1 tablespoon margarine and put buttered slide down in 13 x 9 inch pyrex dish. Top with ½ of the sausage, ½ of the green chilies, and grated cheese. Mix eggs and sour cream and pour over everything. Add remaining sausage, green chilies, and grated cheese. Put in refrigerator for 8 hours, overnight, or freeze. Let come to room temperature before baking. Bake at 350 degrees, uncovered, about 30 or 40 minutes.
Servings: 12

MEATS

Fried Chicken ~ **Cheryl & Ken Wheat**

A Simple Roast ~ **Stanley Smith, Jr.**

Spicy Hot Chicken & Blue Cheese ~ **Mary & Camden Lewis**

Chicken Enchiladas ~ **Dan Reeves**

Meatloaf ~ **Lorita & George Rogers**

Crusted Blue cheese Fillets with saucer ~ **Jan & Billy Gambrell**

Smothered Yard Bird ~ **Harold Green**

Tamale Pie ~ **Edith & Art Baker**

Jim's Ribs ~ **Orral Anne & Jim Moss**

Barbecued Pulled Pork ~ **Cathy & Gerald Sease**

Meat Pie ~ **Marsha Clark**

Carolina Brisket with Barbecue Sauce ~ **Kathi & Jimmy Mitchell**

Ann's Spaghetti ~ **Ann and Jimmy Hunter**

Preacher's Tailgate Ribs ~ **Myra & Preacher Whitner**

Cockaboose Park Tenderloin ~ **Bill Rentz**

Marinated Beef Tenderloin ~ **Mary Ella Wright**

Party Meat Balls ~ **Billy Canada**

Moroccan Chicken ~ **Hannali & Red Furguson**

Chicken Bog ~ **Mark Lenhart**

Marinated Hawaiian Grilled Chicken Breast ~ **Trish Norris**

Grilled Bahamian Chicken ~ **Hugh Poplin**

Bisquick Chicken ~ **Linda Kaye Schnackenburg**

Breakfast Pizza ~ **Kathy Fulmer**

Can-Do Grilled Chicken ~ **Southern Living**

Chicken Casserole ~ **Cathy Murdough**

Chicken Enchiladas ~ **Linda Kaye Schnackenburg**

Chicken Tetrazzini ~ **Caro & Easton Marchant**

Corn Dog ~ **Duce Staley**

Mom's Chicken Casserole ~ **Gamecock Fan**

Pam's Southern Fried Chicken ~ **Pam**

Prime Rib Dry Rub ~ **Tom Cluver**

Stuffed Shells ~ **Terry Kratofil**

Edwards Tenderloin Marinade ~ **Charlie Hawkins**

THE ULTIMATE TAILGATERS

Chris Fulmer is the founder and president of these 35 rabid Gamecock fans from Aikens that attend every home game and many of the away games as well.

Founded in 1994 they set up shop in the fairgrounds hours before game time and pride themselves in being among the last to leave.

Chris's father started taking Chris to home games in the late 1960's and he has only missed one home game since 1972. Chris has not missed a game, home or away since 1984.

Officially, there are 35 Ultimate Tailgaters members, but there are usually 50 or more under their tents as visitors are always welcome. Two new friends from Massachusetts were added in 1998. They vowed they would bring fresh lobsters with them in 1999. They made good on their promise and brought with them 40 lobsters on their 18 hour trip to Columbia the following year. The ultimate Tailgaters have had steak and fresh lobster on their menu one game a year ever since.

KEN WHEAT
THE MATT DILLON OF COCKS CORNER

The best thing that ever happened to Wheatie is when he cut off his toe in June of 1973.

He had just signed a $7,000 a year contract with the Birmingham Americans in the newly formed World Football League.

Practice was to begin in late June, but with the now departed toe, Ken could not make it. Wheaten was a tenacious competitor and would probably have made the team, but his career had suddenly ended. He was devastated.

Without money, a house or a future, Ken went to work for the Recreation Department. He stayed there for a few years, before moving over to the Keenan Company. And then, finally to Boyd Management where he became President in just a few short years.

COCKS CORNER is just one of many, many successful developments engineered under the guidance of Ken's watchful eye.

Had Wheatie not cut off his toe he probably would have played pro football for five or six years and his salary could have risen to 30 or $40,000.

He and Boyd Management have been ultra successful and his salary is now so high a show dog can't jump over it.

What a difference a toe makes.

Fried Chicken

CHERYL & KEN WHEAT

Soak chicken pieces of choice overnight in salt water. Keep refrigerated.

Heat oil in skillet (I prefer electric skillet)

Place flour, salt, pepper and paprika in zip lock bag. Shake to mix.

Place chicken pieces in flour bag after shaking off excess water. Shake bag to coat chicken.

Place in hot oil. Brown on both sides cover and cook covered 30 minutes. Remove lid and continue to fry about 15 more minutes. Turning to get nice crust on both sides.

Drain on paper towel.

Store in plastic container layering brown paper such a new lunch bags torn open or parchment paper. This prevents sogginess.

A Simple Roast

STANLEY SMITH, JR.

3 lb. (2½ to 4) Eye of the Round Beef
1 can French Onion Soup
1 can Golden Mushroom Soup
1 2 qt. covered cast iron round porcelain container

Place Roast in container. Sear all sides of Roast under Hot Heat. Set over at 250 degrees

Mix soup in separate bowl. Pour soup mix over and under Roast. Place in oven

Set timer at 4 hours

CAMDEN LEWIS

Cam is a native West Virginian and the son of legendary Mountaineer coach Art "Pappy" Lewis. Pappy was a two fisted fireball who frequently and physically whipped opposing coaches who came into his state to recruit his boys. Not many players ever left the state.

Cam quarterbacked the Army team that lost to Roger Staubach's Navy team in 1962.

In 1969 Cam joined Paul Dietzel and coached under him for three years while attending law school. Cam is now a practicing attorney in Columbia.

Spicy Hot Chicken & Bleu Cheese En Papillote

MARY & A. CAMDEN LEWIS

4 (4oz.) boned skinned chicken breast halves
3 tablespoons Tabasco sauce
1 cup diagonally sliced carrots
¼ cup thinly sliced green onions
¼ cup sliced mushrooms or zucchini
1 tablespoon Chablis or other dry white wine
1 (2oz.) jar diced pimento, drained
2 tablespoon (1oz.) Crumbled Bleu cheese
Pam cooking spray

CONTINUED

Flatten chicken to ¼" thickness. Pour hot sauce over chicken and cover; marinate 15 minutes in refrigerator.

Cut four (15" x 14") pieces of parchment paper; fold in half crosswise, creasing firmly. Trim each into a heart shape—unfold hearts and place on baking sheets.

Drain chicken, discarding marinade.

Place one chicken breast half on each heart near crease. Combine vegetables with pimento and wine in small bowl; spoon evenly over chicken.

Sprinkle with Bleu cheese.

Fold over remaining half of each heart. Starting with rounded edge, pleat and crimp edges together to seal.

Twist ends tightly to seal. Spray top of each heart with Pam.

Bake at 400 degrees for 12 to 15 minutes or till puffed and lightly browned. Place on individual serving plates and cut open. Serve immediately
Servings: 4, about 180 calories per serving.

DAN REEVES

Played quarterback for Marvin Bass at Carolina. Running back and player-coach for the Dallas Cowboys. Head coach of the Denver Brocos, New York Giants and Atlanta Falcons. Dan is resting this year, but I've got a hunch he's not through coaching.

Chicken Enchiladas
DAN REEVES

Quick fry flour tortillas

FILLING
2 lb. cooked chicken in bite size pieces
½ lb. grated cheddar cheese
½ can chopped green chilies
Garlic powder, salt & pepper

SAUCE
1 pt. sour cream
1 onion
½ can chopped green chilies
1 can cream mushroom soup
1 cream chicken soup
Garlic powder; salt & pepper

Fill fried tortillas with chicken mix. Roll up. Pour sauce over. Top with ½ lb. grated cheddar (or Jack).
Bake at 350 degrees ½ to 1 hour.

GEORGE ROGERS

All American, Heisman Trophy winner. Number one pick in the 1981 NFL draft. Rookie of the Year, winner of the Super Bowl ring, and all around good guy. George Rogers has done it all. He is simply the greatest football player in the history of our school, *until Clowney*

Meatloaf
LORITA & GEORGE RODGERS

1 pound ground beef
1 green pepper
½ red pepper
½ yellow pepper
2 eggs
Shake and bake
1 Lifton Onion Soup

Mix together and shape. Cook for 1½ hours and let set.

BILLY GAMBRELL

Billy was a three year letterman at Carolina and also lettered in track. He played 7 years in the NFL with St. Louis Cardinals and Detroit Lions, and played briefly in the Canadian League

I met Billy at a party one night after my senior year. Both of us had a cocktail or two and Billy stated flatly "I'm going to break every record you have at this school." "Have at it," I replied. To my knowledge I've never held a record. We've been great friends ever since.

Crusted Blue Cheese Fillets with Yummy Mushroom Sauce
JAN & BILLY GAMBRELL

SAUCE
1 stick butter
4 – 6 cloves garlic, chopped
1 large shallot or onion, sliced or chopped
1 cup sliced mushrooms
1 tablespoon chopped fresh thyme
¾ cup beef broth (can or from cubes)
½ cup wine (dry red), but any kind will do.

Melt butter in heavy skillet over medium heat. Sauté the garlic, shallot, mushrooms and thyme until tender (3-5 Minutes) Add broth and wine. Heat until sauce is reduced to about ½ cup—about 10 to 12 minutes and set aside.

CRUSTY BLUE CRUMBS
½ cup blue cheese crumbs (2-3oz. cheese)
1 cup of seasoned croutons (crushed in Ziploc) or
  ½ to ¾ bread crumbs or Japanese Panko
1 tbs. fresh chopped parsley

CONTINUED

With fork, mix together well and set aside.

Prepare fillets: to your own desired doneness. We take 3 or 4 inch fillets and heat butter in black skillet, salt & pepper steak and fry. Heat each side. We like medium rare to rare.

Remove Fillets from skillet and place in baking pan or pan suitable for serving.

Cover with crusty blue crumbs and then yummy mushroom sauce. Broil for 2 to 3 minutes or until toasty and bubbly.

Smothered "Yard Bird"
HAROLD GREEN

1 2-to 3-lb. chicken, cup up
1 cup all-purpose flour
¼ teaspoon garlic powder
½ teaspoon onion powder
1½ teaspoons seasoned salt
2 teaspoons pepper
½ cup bacon drippings or vegetable shortening
1 small onion, diced
1¼ cups hot water
½ cup half and half

Wash chicken. Combine flour and next 4 ingredients and coat chicken; shake off excess. Reserve any leftover seasoned flour, recoat chicken, and refrigerate 1 hr. In a large, heavy frying pan over medium-high heat, melt drippings or shortening. Shortening is sufficiently hot when a haze forms above it and a drop of water can dance across its surface. Reduce heat to medium, add chicken, and fry until the chicken is golden on all sides.

Remove chicken to a paper towel-covered platter.

Remove all but ¼ cup of the reserved seasoned flour and brown it until dark golden. Add the hot water and half and half to the pan. Stir until smooth. Then return chicken to pan. Cover tightly and simmer over low heat until tender, approx. 25 to 30 minutes.

Serve for breakfast with grits and biscuits or at dinner with rice, biscuits, and yams.

Tamale Pie
EDITH & ART BAKER

1 small onion or dried onion
1 green pepper, chopped
1 lb. ground beef
½ lb. ground pork sausage
3½ cups tomatoes
2½ can whole kernel corn
1 tsp. salt
2 tsp. chili powder
1 cup corn meal, self-rising
2 eggs, well beaten
2 cups cheese, grated

Brown beef and sausage, add dried onion, pepper, tomatoes, corn, salt, chili powder. Simmer for 20 minutes. Pour into large shallow baking dish. Mix meal, milk and eggs; pour over meat mixture. Sprinkle with cheese.

Bake at 350 degrees for 45 to 50 minutes. Can be made the day before.

JIM MOSS

Jim was a three year letterman and a two-time All-ACC player for Carolina in 1961,62. He was a two-time winner of the Jacobs Blocking Trophy.

Jim Boy's Show Off Ribs
ORRAL ANNE & JIM MOSS

If you're one of those who like to bring the little grill along, this is for you.

Baby back ribs, as many as you want
Black pepper
Finger sucking Bar-B-Que sauce (or your choice)

Sprinkle ribs with pepper on both sides. Put in deep

large pan, cover with foil, and air tight. Bake 3 hours. Drain juice off and rewrap ribs for traveling.

Ribs are cooked so just put sauce of your choice on and brown on both sides. Take plenty of napkins.

Babecued Pulled Pork
CATHY & GERALD SEASE

1 boneless pork butt, about 4 lbs.
3 tbsp. dark brown sugar
2 tbsp. Emeril's Essence
1 tbs. salt
1 tbsp. cumin
1 tbsp paprika
1 tbsp. black pepper, freshly ground
1 tbsp. cayenne
Wet Mop Basting Sauce
Barbeque Sauce

WET MOP BASTING SAUCE
1 cup white vinegar
1 cup apple cider vinegar
1 tbsp. dark brown sugar
1 tbsp. red pepper flakes
1 tbsp. cracked black pepper
1 tbsp. salt

BARBEQUE SAUCE
1 cup apple cider vinegar
1 cup ketchup
3 tbsp. packed brown sugar
1 tbsp. yellow mustard
1 tbsp. molasses
1 tsp. salt
½ tsp dried crushed red pepper

CONTINUED

Place pork in baking dish. In bowl, combine sugar, Essence, salt, cumin, paprika, pepper and cayenne. Rub the seasoning evenly over the pork to coat. Cover with plastic and refrigerate at least 4 hours or overnight.

Preheat oven or smoker to 225 degrees.

Bring pork to room temperature and place in roasting pan, fat side up. Slow cook in oven, basting with met mop basting sauce every 45 minutes until tender and internal temperature reaches 160 degrees. Cooking time is 6 to 7 hours. Remove from oven and let rest for 20 to 30 minutes.

With a knife and fork, pull the meat apart into small slices or chunks. Serve with Barbeque Sauce.

"Hot-Ta-Meat" Pies
MARSHA CLARK
COURTESY OF STUART WHATLEY

FILLING
2 tbsp. flour
1 tbsp. shortening
½ lb. ground beef
1½ lbs. ground pork
2 large dry onions, chopped
6 green onions, chopped
4 tbsp. parsley, chopped

Make a roux of shortening and flour; add other ingredients and salt and pepper to taste. Cook thoroughly and let cool before placing in dough.

PASTRY
4 cups flour
2 eggs
½ cup melted shortening
Milk

2 tsp. baking powder
Salt and pepper to taste.

Sift flour and baking powder, add shortening, then eggs. Add enough milk to make a stiff dough. Roll very thin. Use a saucer to cut circles of dough same size as saucer.

Fill half full with meat mixture. Fold dough over, dampen edges with water and crimp with fork. Fry in deep fat until golden brown. (Some people prefer to reverse the proportions of beef and pork.) (P.S.) I reverse the portions and add cayenne pepper and hot sauce.

Carolina Brisket with Barbecue Sauce
KATHI & JIMMY MITCHELL

1½ teaspoon salt
1½ teaspoon pepper
2 tablespoons chili powder
1 teaspoon crushed bay leaves
2 tablespoons liquid smoke
4 lbs. beef brisket

BARBECUE SAUCE
3 tablespoons brown sugar
1 14 oz. bottle ketchup
½ cut water
2 tablespoons liquid smoke
Salt and pepper to taste
4 tablespoons Worcestershire sauce
2 teaspoons dry mustard
2 teaspoons celery seed
6 tablespoons butter
¼ teaspoons cayenne pepper

For Brisket: Combine salt, pepper, chili powder and bay leaves. Rub meat completely with liquid smoke. Place meat, fat side up, in a large roasting pan. Sprinkle dry seasoning mixture on top. Cover tightly. Bake for 4 hours at 325 degrees. Scrape seasoning off meat and cut in very thin slices across the grain.

Serve with barbecue sauce.

For Barbecue Sauce: Combine all ingredients. Bring to a boil, stirring occasionally. Cook for 10 minutes. Serve with brisket on onion rolls.

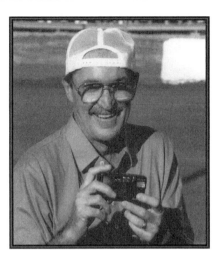

JIMMY HUNTER

A native of South Carolina Jimmy earned three football and two baseball letters at Carolina.

His real love was racing and life. Work hard and play hard was his motto and he did just that. The work often over shadowed by the play.

After college he took a job as a sportswriter in Columbia. NASCAR was then in its infancy and not much coverage was devoted to it.

He wrote for 4 or 5 years for the State paper until a public relations job opened at Darlington raceway. His job was to entertain the press and news media. Jimmy knew how to entertain.

After two years at Darlington he returned to writing. This time with the Atlanta Journal Constitution.

In 1975 a public relations job opened up at the Talladega Raceway so it was back to entertaining. After two or three shaky years at Talladega, on the day of the race, Jimmy went to work early, worked too hard and totaled the pace car. The work and play had finally overlapped to an embarrassing degree.

"It's the bottle or your job he was told," and damn him, he took the job. He quit drinking and hasn't touched a drop in the 27 years since.

In 1981 he moved to Daytona Beach. Two years later he was promoted to Vice President of

CONTINUED

Administrations for NASCAR.

In 1993 Jimmy was President of Darlington Raceway.

In 1995 Jimmy was awarded the Order of The Palmetto, South Carolina's highest civic honor and was named South Carolina's Tourism Ambassador of the year.

Jimmy is currently Vice President of Corporate Communications for NASCAR.

Damn him, I miss my old drinking buddy.

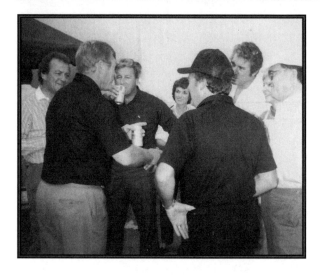

Ann's Spaghetti Sauce

ANN & JIMMY HUNTER

2 lbs ground beef
4 onions chopped
1 large bell pepper chopped
1 large jar sliced mushrooms
Salt
Pepper
Garlic powder
Italian seasoning
1 large jar Prego or Ragu traditional spaghetti sauce
1 small can tomato sauce
2 large cans diced tomatoes
¼ cup worcestershire sauce
1 large jar sliced mushrooms

Brown ground beef in a large pot. Add chopped onions and bell pepper and let all of this simmer. Add salt, pepper, garlic powder to taste. Add diced tomatoes, Italian seasoning, jar of sauce, tomatoe paste, and mushrooms. Let this simmer a while and then add worcestershire sauce. I think the secret to a great sauce is letting it simmer for at least 3 or 4 hours. I like to serve this over angle hair pasta.

Preacher's Tailgate Ribs

MYRNA & PREACHER WHITNER

6 to 10 racks of Pork Baby Back Ribs (Danish if available)
A rack consists of 12 to 14 ribs.
Honey
Dried Lipton's Onion Soup Mix

Cut racks in half between center. Parboil ribs for 5 to 7 minutes. Remove and pat dry with paper towels.

Coat meaty side (top) of ribs with honey and rub honey over entire top of ribs.

Sprinkle dried onion soup mix (approx. one pack per rack) over honey coated side of ribs.

Place ribs (with honey and soup side up) on grill and cook (over indirect heat) until crisp, but not burned. Turn once to cook both sides crisp.

Remove, when done, and slice racks into individual ribs. Refrigerates and freezes well

Cockaboose Pork Tenderloin

BILL RENTZ

You can use the tenderloin or the loin for this recipe. The tenderloin is smaller and much tenderer. Tenderloin is my preference. Salt and pepper the loins to taste and cook on Charcoal grill. Gas grill is ok, if you do not use charcoal.

Cook until well done, but do not dry out the meat. Try to leave moist inside. Sauce is made from pineapple preserves, Kikkoman soy sauce and sesame seeds.

Mix the sauce ingredients using ¾ tablespoon of soy per small jar of pineapple preserves. Shake in a generous portion of sesame seeds and mix with a spoon. I usually make extra sauce because; this is the hit for most people.

When the meat is 10 to 15 minutes from being cooked, brush the sauce on the top. Do not turn as it will burn the sauce. I like to place more sauce on entire tenderloin when I take it off the grill.

Serve with the sauce on the side. If using as a heavy appetizer, place a plate of silver dollar size French bread along side of the meat and the sauce.

Marinated Beef Tenderloin

MARY ELLA WRIGHT

2 beef tenderloins, trimmed (4 to 5 lbs. each)
Marinade:
½ cup Wishbone Italian Dressing
2 tsp. soy sauce
1 tbls. Worcestershire
½ cup red wine
1 tbls. garlic, minced
1 tbls. thyme or rosemary
1 tsp. coarse ground black pepper
Red pepper to taste

Mix marinade ingredients and pour over tenderloins.

Cover and refrigerate for at least 8 hours, turning once. Allow tenderloins to come to room temperature before roasting. Preheat oven to 500 degrees.

Remove tenderloins from marinade and place in shallow roasting pan. Cook for 11 to 12 minutes per pound for rare (130 degrees on meat thermometer) 140 for medium.

Roast beef should rest 15 to 20 minutes before carving.

Party Meat Balls

BILLY CANADA

1 small onion, chopped
1 lb. ground beef
2 cups cracker crumbs
2 eggs
1½ tsp. salt
Pinch of pepper

CONTINUED

1½ cups green pepper, well chopped
1½ cups red pepper, well chopped
Garlic to taste
1 tablespoon parsley
¼ teaspoon thyme
1 tablespoon red wine
¾ cup tomato juice or V8

Mix beef with crumbs. Mix in next 9 ingredients. Shape into balls. Brown in butter. Place in casserole. Add wine and tomato juice. Cover. Bake 1 hour and 30 minutes to 2 hours at 325 degrees.

Moroccan Chicken
HANNALI & RED FURGUSON

Hope you find these mouthwatering and practical. Red loves them all. I know, because I've captured his heart through the burners on the kitchen stove and though his stomach!

2 tbsp. flour
1½ tsp. ground coriander
½ tsp. ground red pepper
¼ tsp. salt
¼ tsp ground cinnamon
1 lb. skinned boned chicken breast, cut into 1-inch pieces
2 tsp. olive oil
¾ cup raisins
1 tsp. ground turmeric
Cooking spray
¼ cup sliced almonds, toasted
¼ Cup plain yogurt
¼ cup chopped fresh cilantro

Combine first 6 ingredients; reserve tbsp. of mixture. Add chicken to flour mixture and toss to coat. Heat oil in large skillet. Add chicken, cook 5 minutes, stirring frequently. Stir in broth, raisins, and turmeric, bring to boil; reduce heat, simmer for 8 minutes, until chicken is cooked and slightly thickened.

Serve with polenta, pasta, rice and condiments. Can serve as an appetizer with tooth picks.

Chicken Bog
MARK LENHART

They scrape the bottom of the pot every time I make this (it is my father's recipe handed down, he has passed away). You will need a pot big enough to hold 20 cups rice. (You can make less I guess, but why would you want to? After all we are tailgating.

5 whole chickens, washed
3 lbs. thick sliced bacon
3 lbs. ground spicy hot sausage
1 jar chicken bouillon powder type
8 Vidalia onions, chopped
1 stalk celery, chopped
1 cup Texas Pete
½ cup Worcestershire sauce
Salt and pepper to taste
4 sticks butter

In a large pot add 45 cups water, whole chickens and jar of bouillon, boil till chicken can be pulled off the bone easily. While chicken is boiling fry bacon and brown sausage, set aside.

After chicken is cooked tender take out of pot, pick all meat off bones and put meat back in pot with broth left from boiling chickens.

Now add onion, celery, bacon, sausage, Texas Pete and Worcestershire sauce and butter. Bring back to a boil; you can now add rice about 17 to 20 cups. (depending how much broth has evaporated) make sure to add rice slowly and stir as to get mixture mixed into the rice. Now cover and let set till rice is tender.

I make the broth the day before and take the pot to the game then all I have to do is bring pot to boil and add rice at game, so it's hot and fresh. Also have extra Texas Pete and Worcestershire sauce, so you can KICK IT UP A NOTCH like the FIGHTING COCKS.
Servings: A lot

Marinated Hawiian Grilled Chicken Breasts
TRISH NORRIS

½ cup reduced-sodium soy sauce
½ cup unsweetened crush pineapple, with juice
¼ cup vegetable oil
½ cup brown sugar
2 teaspoons ground ginger
1 teaspoon dry mustard
¼ teaspoon freshly ground pepper
6 to 8 boneless, skinned chicken breast

Combine first 8 ingredients in a plastic zip lock bag and mix. Add chicken breasts and marinate over night. Grill at medium heat for approx. six to eight minutes on both sides. When we tailgate, I carry the chicken in a small cooler by itself and throw the zip lock bag away when finished. We have a traveling gas grill that we use to cook the chicken breast.

Grilled Bahamian Chicken
HUGH POPLIN

2 jalapeno peppers, minced
¼ cup fresh cilantro, minced
1 (14 oz.) can coconut milk
2 tablespoons fresh lime juice
4 skinned and boned chicken breast halves

Whisk together first 4 ingredients.

Cut chicken into 1-inch-side strips, and place in a shallow dish; add milk mixture. Cover and chill 1 to 2 hours. Soak 16 (6-inch) wooden skewers in water 15 minutes.

Drain chicken, covered with grill lid, over medium-high heat (350 to 400) turning often, 4 to 6 minutes or until done. This is wonderful with the Cock's Kickin Mango Salsa.
Servings: 4

Cocky's Kickin Mango Salsa
HUGH POPLIN

½ cup chopped tomato
1 to 2 jalapeno peppers, minced
½ cup chopped purple onion
2 tablespoons fresh lime juice
½ cup chopped mango
½ teaspoon chili powder
¼ cup chopped green bell pepper
1 tablespoon honey

Combine all ingredients. Cover & chill 3 hrs. Serve with chicken or pork. Our family loves it anytime.

Bisquick Chicken
LINDA KAYE SCHNACKENBERG

6 tbls. Oleo or butter
⅔ cup Bisquick
1½ tsp. paprika
1¼ tsp. salt
¼ tsp. pepper

Heat oven to 425 degrees. Melt butter and coat chicken. Mix ingredients and coat chicken.

Place skin side down for 35 minutes. Turn and back 15 minutes or until juices run clear.
Servings: 6 to 8

Breakfast Pizza
KATHY FULMER

1 lb. sausage
1 package crescent rolls
1 cup frozen, loose, hash brown potatoes
1 cup shredded cheddar cheese
5 eggs
¼ cup milk
½ teaspoon pepper
½ teaspoon salt
2 tablespoons parmesan cheese

*Cook sausage and drain. Place dough in ungreased 12"
pizza pan with the points to the center. Press the edges
together to seal. Spoon sausage over and sprinkle with
the potatoes. Top with cheddar cheese. Beat the rest
together and pour onto the crust. Sprinkle with parmesan cheese. Bake at 375 degrees for 25 to 30 minutes.*

Can-Do Grilled Chicken
SOUTHERN LIVING, STEVEN RAICHLEN

Basic Beer-Can Chicken
2 tablespoon All-Purpose Barbecue Rub, divided
1 (3½ to 4 lb.) whole chicken
1 tablespoon vegetable oil
1 (12 oz.) can beer

*Sprinkle 1 teaspoon All-Purpose Barbecue Rub inside
body cavity and ½ teaspoon inside neck cavity of
chicken. Rub oil over skin. Sprinkle with 1 tablespoon
All-Purpose Barbecue Rub, and rub over skin.*

*Pour out half of beer (about ¾ cup), and reserve for
another use, leaving remaining beer in can, make 2
additional holes in top of can. Spoon remaining 1 ½
teaspoons rub into beer can. Beer will start to foam.*

*Place chicken upright onto the beer can, fitting
can into cavity. Pull legs forward to form a tripod,
allowing chicken to stand upright.*

*Prepare a fire by piling charcoal on one side of grill,
leaving other side empty. (For gas grills, light only one
side.) Place a drip pan on unlit side, and place food
grate on grill. Place chicken upright over drip pan.
Grill, covered with grill lid, 1 hr. & 15 minutes or until
golden and a meat thermometer registers 180 degrees.*

*Remove chicken from grill and let stand 5 min-
utes; carefully remove can.*

ALL-PURPOSE BARBECUE RUB
¼ cup coarse salt
¼ cup dark brown sugar
½ cup sweet paprika
2 tablespoons pepper
Combine all ingredients. Store mixture in an airtight
jar, away from heat, up to 6 months.

Cola-Can Chicken

2 tablespoons Barbecue Rub, divided
1 (3½ to 4 lb) whole chicken
3 tablespoons vegetable oil
1 (12oz.) can cola
Cola Barbecue Sauce

Sprinkle 1 teaspoon Barbecue Rub inside body cavity and ½ teaspoon inside neck cavity of chicken.

Rub oil over skin. Sprinkle with 1 tablespoon Barbecue Rub and rub over skin.

Pour out half of cola (about ¼ cup). And reserve for Cola Barbecue Sauce, leaving remaining cola in can. Makes 2 additional holes in top of can. Spoon remaining 1½ teaspoons rub into cola can. Cola will start to foam.

Place chicken upright into the cola can, fitting can into cavity. Pull legs forward to form a tripod, allowing chicken to stand upright.

Prepare a fire by piling charcoal on one side of grill, leaving other side empty. (For gas grills, light only one side.) Place a drip pan on unlit side and place food grate on grill. Place chicken upright over drip pan. Grill, covered with grill lid, 1 hr. & 15 minutes or until golden and meat thermometer registers 180 degrees.

Remove chicken from grill, and let stand 5 minutes; carefully remove can. Serve with Cola Barbecue Sauce

BARBECUE RUB
1 tablespoon mild chili powder
2 teaspoons salt
2 teaspoons light brown sugar
1 teaspoon pepper
1 teaspoon ground cumin
½ teaspoon garlic powder
¼ teaspoon ground red pepper
Combine all ingredients.

COLA BARBECUE SAUCE
1 tablespoon butter
½ small onion, minced
1 tablespoon minced fresh ginger
1 garlic clove, minced
¾ cup reserved cola
¾ cup ketchup
½ teaspoon grated lemon rind
2 tablespoons fresh lemon juice
2 tablespoons steak sauce
½ teaspoon liquid smoke
½ teaspoon pepper
Salt to taste

Melt butter in a heavy saucepan over medium heat. Add onion, ginger and garlic; sauce 3 minutes or until tender.

Stir in reserved cola; bring mixture to a boil. Stir in ketchup and remaining ingredients; bring to a boil. Reduce heat, and simmer 5 minutes.

Note for testing purposes only, we used A1 Steak Sauce.

Servings: 2 to 4

Quick & Easy Chicken Casserole
CATHY MURDAUGH

1 cup Minute rice
1 can Cream of Chicken Soup
½ cup milk
2 5oz.cans white meat boned chicken
1 cup shredded cheddar cheese
20 to 30 saltines
Stick of butter or margarine

Cook rice according to package directions. Pour into 2 qt. casserole dish. Add soup, milk, and chicken to rice, stir. Sprinkle crushed saltines on top of cheese and dot with butter. Cook at 325 degrees for 30 minutes.

Chicken Enchiladas
LINDA KAYE SCHNACKENBERG

2 cups diced chicken
2 cups (8ozs.) shredded Monterey Jack cheese
1 can (2¼ oz.) sliced ripe olives, drained
2 tsp. dried parsley flakes
½ tsp. garlic powder
½ tsp. salt
⅛ tsp. pepper
6 to 8 flour tortillas (8" size)

SAUCE
1 medium onion, diced
½ green pepper, diced
1 tbls. cooking oil

Cook on low 6 to 8 hours or on high 3 to 4 hrs. until chicken is cooked through. Excellent with rice.

Chicken Tetrazzini a la Caro
CARO & EASTON MARCHANT

1 8 oz. package spaghetti
1 cup onion, chopped
1 cup celery, chopped
½ cup green pepper, chopped
½ lb. sharp cheese, grated
1 cup chicken broth
3 cups cooked chicken or turkey, cut into strips
1 8 oz. can mushrooms
2 10¾ oz. cans cream of mushroom soup
Sherry (optional)

Sauté onions, celery, and pepper until soft. Cook spaghetti in chicken broth as directed on package. Mix all ingredients and put into a 9 x 13 casserole dish. Sprinkle grated cheese on top. Cook, covered, for 30 minutes at 375 degrees. Then cook uncovered until cheese is melted.

A wonderful make-ahead recipe to serve after the game or to freeze and take on trips.

Corn Dogs
DUCE STALEY

Jumbo long hot dogs, package
⅔ cup cornmeal
1 cup plain flour
1½ teaspoons baking powder
1 teaspoon salt
2 tablespoons fat
1 egg
¾ cup sweet milk

Cut fat into dry ingredients, and then add egg and milk. Skewer wieners and dip into mixture. Take skewer wieners and roast over open bed of coals or deep fry at 325 degrees.

Mom's Chicken Casserole
UNKNOWN

8 chicken breasts
2 cans of cream of chicken soup
1 cup of sour cream
¾ cup milk
2 tablespoons margarine or butter
1 pkg. bread crumbs

Boil chicken until tender. Remove skin. Pull chicken off the bone, and salt. Mix chicken, sour cream, and butter. Place mixture into casserole dish. Pour in milk and cream of chicken soup. Sprinkle bread crumbs on top. Bake covered at 350 degrees for 45 minutes, or bake uncovered at 350 degrees for 15 minutes.

Pam's Southern Fried Chicken
PAM

1 fryer (cut into serving size pieces) or 6 boneless
  chicken breasts
2 to 4 cups of buttermilk
4 cups of sifted self-rising flour
Salt and pepper to taste
Crisco or cooking oil

Wash chicken and salt and pepper. In a large bowl, layer chicken pouring buttermilk covering each level and completely covering all. Refrigerate overnight.

Place flour in gallon size (or larger) plastic zip-lock bag. Dip or shake each chicken piece in flour until thoroughly covered. Place chicken in deep skillet or Fry Daddy containing medium/hot Crisco. Fry uncovered until golden brown on both sides. Make sure chicken is not crowded while frying. Drain well and serve. Note: Crisco should be very deep to properly fry the chicken.

GRAVY (OPTIONAL)

Approximately ¾ cup of milk and ¼ cup of evaporated milk room temperature.

After frying chicken, leave approx. 1 cup of Crisco/oil in skillet on medium setting. Sift 1 cup of flour and slowly place 1 tablespoon at a time into

CONTINUED

skillet stirring frequently. Mixture should be at least half and half with a little more liquid than flour. Add salt and pepper. Cook until mixture has thickened; and turned somewhat "paper sack tan." Heat may be raised to achieve. Add milk mixture and stir. Water and or a small amount of butter may be added for better consistency and taste.

Prime Rib "Dry Rub"
TOM CULVER

1 cup + 2 teaspoons salt
¼ cup + 3½ teaspoons black pepper
¼ cup + 2 teaspoons garlic powder
¼ cup + 1 teaspoon accent
3 teaspoons paprika
1 cup + 2 teaspoons Sugar

Stuffed Shells
TERRY KRATOFIL

2 lbs. ground round
½ small onion, chopped
½ 10 oz. box frozen spinach, thawed & squeeze dry
2 eggs
1 cup parmesan cheese
1 large jar spaghetti sauce of choice
1 box jumbo shells
1 cup mozzarella cheese, shredded
Salt and pepper to taste

Cook the shells following directions on the box. Drain, rinse, and set aside to cool.

Put the ground round in a pan along with the onions and cook until browned. Drain the meat and put in a large bowl. Add squeezed spinach, eggs, parmesan cheese, salt and pepper. Mix all of this together and put in refrigerator to cool. Open jar of sauce. Get a 9 x 12 baking dish and put about 3 tablespoons of sauce on bottom. Then get the meat mix and shells. Open shells and fill with mixture. Place in the baking dish and when dish is full, spoon sauce on the top of shells, sprinkle with some parmesan and sprinkle mozzarella cheese on top. Cover and bake at 350 degrees for 25 minutes or until hot inside.

These can be made a day ahead and baked before going tailgating. I cook these before I leave and put them in an insulated carrier and they stay hot until we are ready to eat.
Servings: A box makes about 30 shells

Edwards Tenderloin Marinade
COURTESY OF CHARLIE HAWKINS

¼ to ½ cup soy sauce
¼ cup olive oil
1 teas. Minced garlic
1 tbl. Dijon mustard
¼ cup Teriyaki sauce
2 Tbls. Brown sugar
Juice of 1 lemon

Put above ingredients in a jar. Shake till well mixed. Marinate meat overnight in bag in refrigerator.

Grill until 160 degrees. I substitute the brown sugar and use Hoi sin Chinese Sauce.

SEAFOOD

Beaufort Stew ~ Gene Ransdale & Eddie Elmore

Old Post Office Crab Cakes ~ Philip Bardin & David Gressette

Fish & Shrimp Casserole ~ Melvin Wright

Marinated Lemon Shrimp ~ Mary Ella Wright

Seafood Chowder ~ Al Johnson

Creole Shrimp ~ Billy Canada

Bobby's Seafood Gumbo ~ Robert Mitchell

Carolina Crab Cakes ~ Hugh Poplin

Steamed Oyster ~ Bright Stevenson

Barbecued Shrimp ~ Cathy & Gerald Sease

Shrimp and Dumplings ~ Pappy Poston

Shrimp Scampi Sauce ~ Okeechobee Steak House

College Shrimp ~ Zoe & Alex Sanders

Crab Imperial ~ Tom Price

Deviled Crab ~ Jim Guest

Marinated Shrimp Medley ~ Susie & Heyward King

Shrimp and Grits ~ Phil Petty

Smoked Salmon Rolls ~ Becky & Rick Wallace

Soft Shell Crab ~ Scott Kyle

GENE RANSDALE & EDDIE ELMORE

Gene was raised in Denmark, S.C. and educated in New York City and brings a formal, elegant and sophistication to tailgating. Gene gives a new meaning when it comes to tailgating with style. Eddie, Gene's cohort in tailgating was born during his father's senior year at Carolina and raised a Gamecock but screwed up and decided to graduate from Florida State. But both love to tailgate at Carolina games when they get a chance.

Frogmore, Beaufort, Low Country Boil Stew

EDDIE ELMORE & GENE RANSDALE

3lbs medium shrimp or frozen boiled shrimp
¼ lb butter
2 lbs mild Hillshire Sausage (cut in small slices)

5 ears of corn (cut in two) or Green Giant frozen cut ears
2 lbs medium new red potatoes (diced in large pieces)
1 large onion
4 TBS Old Bay Seasoning or 1 bag crab boil
4 tps salt

In a 6-8 quart pot or larger fill the pot half with water, add butter, salt, crab boil, sausage and onions. Bring to a boil. Add corn and potatoes, stir and bring to a boil for 4 minutes add shrimp and stir for 4 to 6 minutes, or until shrimp start floating to the top of water. Remove from heat and let sit for about 5 minutes. With a large slotted spoon place ingredients in a large bowl or place in the middle of a table on newspaper. Serve with hot butter dip and seafood cocktail sauce
Servings: 5 to 6 people

Old Post Office Crab Cakes

CHEF PHILIP BARDIN

David Gressette (grandson of Tatum) and Philip Bardin, childhood friends, opened the Old Post Office restaurant at Edisto Island in 1988.

Folding in the egg whites give these cakes the buoyancy of soufflé. Baking, rather than frying, abets their fluffiness.

- 1 lb. jumbo lump crabmeat
- 1 lb. claw crabmeat1 cup high quality mayonnaise (Hellmann's) is a good one.
- ¼ cup Dijon mustard
- 1 Tablespoon Old Bay Seasoning
- Juice of 1 lemon
- 1 cup panko (Japanese breadcrumbs)
- 2 egg whites, stiffly beaten

Preheat the oven to 475 degrees. Make sure there are no shells in the crabmeat and that the meat is moist but not watery. Gently mix the crabmeats, mayonnaise, mustard, Old Bay, lemon juice, and panko, being careful not to break up the lump crabmeat too much. Fold in the beaten egg whites. Using about a 4 ounce ice cream scoop, scoop out cakes onto an oiled baking sheet. You can make large or small cakes. Bake for 12 to 15 minutes until the cakes are fluffy and golden. Serve with Mousseline Sauce. This can make as many as 20 cakes depending on your scoop size. Half or quarter the recipe if you do not want that many, but I suggest making and holding a big batch. This mixture holds very well for several days in the refrigerator. If you omit the egg whites, you have a respectable crab salad. Servings: 4

Fish and Shrimp Casserole

MELVIN WRIGHT

Melvin is Executive Vice President of Maintenance at Riverbend Plantation

- 1 cup dry white wine
- 12 medium size shrimp
- 2 tablespoons butter
- 4 green onions, finely chopped
- 1½ cups heavy cream
- 1 tablespoon Cajun spices (see below)
- ½ teaspoon dried basil
- ¼ teaspoon sweet paprika
- 1¼ pounds white fish fillets
- 2 teaspoons dry mustard

CONTINUED

½ cup olive oil
2 tablespoons butter
2 cups cooked rice

In a saucepan bring wine to a boil; add shrimp and simmer until just tender. Remove shrimp. Peel and devein. Reserve wine.

In same pan cook onions in butter for 1 minute. Add cream, half the Cajun spices, basil and paprika. Bring to boil. Add wine and shrimp; simmer 1 to 3 minutes. Season fish fillets with remaining Cajun spices and mustard. Heat oil and butter in a large skillet. Add fish and cook 3 to 5 minutes on each side. Slice into even pieces. Place rice in an oven-proof dish.

Arrange fish on top and cover with sauce. Bake at 400 degrees for 10 minutes.

CAJUN SPICES
1 tablespoon garlic powder
1 tablespoon onion powder
2 teaspoons white pepper
2 teaspoons cracked black pepper
1½ teaspoons cayenne pepper
2 teaspoons dried oregano

Mix the spices together and store in a spice jar
Cajun spices makes meat, pork and chicken taste better.
I also serve Texas Pete along with the plate of Fish and Shrimp Casserole.

Marinated Lemon Shrimp
MARY ELLA WRIGHT

2 lbs. shrimp
3 cups beer
1 cup water
1 tsp. salt
⅔ cup oil
½ cup white tarragon vinegar
¼ cup fresh chopped parsley
1½ tsp pepper
Dash Tabasco
2 onions sliced very thin
2 lemons sliced very thin
2 tbs. capers with liquid

Boil shrimp in beer, water, salt. Drain shrimp and peel. In a small jar with lid, combine oil, vinegar, parsley, salt, pepper, and Tabasco. Cover and shake well. In a large bowl alternate layers of shrimp, onion slices, lemon slices and capers. Pour oil and vinegar mixture over all and marinate in refrigerator at least 8 hours. Serve with toothpicks.

Seafood Chowder
AL JOHNSON

5 lbs. frozen Cod fillets
2 lbs. Shrimp
1 lb. Bay Scallops
4 6 oz. cans chopped Clams
2 6 oz. cans Crab Meat
6 robs Celery
4 medium Onions

2 tsp. chopped Garlic
2 16 oz. cans New England Clam Chowder
6 18.7 oz. cans Campbell's Cream of Potato Soup
1 cup Flour
1 qt. (approx.) Milk
Dry White Wine

Sauté onions, celery and garlic in butter until soft. Stir in flour, and then add clam juice to make a roux. Add potato soup, clam chowder, clams, crab meat and milk.

Steam cod fillets in wine. When done, break into small pieces and add to chowder. Sauté shrimp in butter and add to chowder. Season to taste.

Servings: Should be enough for 10 to 12 people

Creole Shrimp

BILLY CANADA

Cook enough bacon to get 8 tbsp. drippings, save
  bacon
4 onions
2 bell peppers
2 cups celery
2 qt. can tomatoes
1 tsp. sugar
6 tbsp. tomato paste
Salt and pepper to taste
6 cups cooked shrimp

Cut up onions, pepper and celery. Cook in bacon drippings 10 to 15 minutes. Add tomatoes, sugar and paste. Let simmer slowly to think consistency for 30 to 45 minutes. Add salt and pepper 15 minutes before serving. Add cooked shrimp. Serve over rice and bacon.

Bobby's Seafood Gumbo

BOBBY MITCHELL
BOBBY IS PRESIDENT OF BERKELEY COUNTY
GAMECOCK CLUB

This recipe makes enough to fill a large crock-pot.

1 cup onion
1 cup bell pepper
1 cup celery
1 cup okra
14 oz. can of beef broth
1 package of beef bouillon
1 can (28 oz.) tomatoes
Salt and pepper to taste
Creole seasoning to taste
1 lb. shrimp, peeled, cut up, uncooked
6 oz. can drab meat, drained
6 oz. can chopped clams, drained
1 cup rice, uncooked

Cut up ¾-1 cup each onions, bell pepper, celery, and okra. In large pot add 2 14 oz. cans of beef broth, one cup beef bouillon and tomatoes. Add veggies.

Add salt, pepper, and creole seasoning.

Bring to boil, then reduce heat, cover and cook until veggies are tender (about 45 minutes).

Turn heat up and add shrimp; crab meat and clams. Cook about 5 minutes.

Add rice. Stir in a cook about 15 minutes.

Turn heat off and let sit a little while. It will thicken and you may need to add some liquid. If needed stir in 1 to 2 cups hot beef bouillon.

Carolina Crab Cakes

HUGH POPLIN

1 cup dried breadcrumbs
2 large eggs, lightly beaten
2 pounds lump crabmeat, picked over for cartilage
½ cup cilantro leaves, fresh and chopped
4 scallions, chopped
1 red pepper, seeded and diced
1 jalapeño pepper, seeded and diced
1 cup mayonnaise
Salt and freshly ground pepper
1 cup vegetable oil for frying

In a large bowl, gently mix together the breadcrumbs, eggs, crabmeat, cilantro, scallions, peppers, mayonnaise, and salt and pepper to taste. Make the crabmeat mixture into 24 small thick cakes, about 2 inches in diameter. Heat the vegetable oil in a large frying pan over medium-high heat, hot, not smoking. Cook the crabmeat for 2 to 3 minutes per side, turn when golden brown. Drain on paper towel before serving.

BRIGHT STEVENSON

I first met Bright in the fall of 1956. Bright owned the Coronet Motel and the Circus Room Night Club in Eastover. The Circus Room had the finest food and the only mixed drinks in the Columbia area at that time.

He called me and invited me down to have dinner on him. I got a date with a girl with a car and went on down.

We hit it off and Bright more or less adopted me from that point on. He said he would pay my fraternity dues and buy me a fraternity pen.

I don't think I've told you but Bright is a little bit crazy. He raced those cigar shaped boats in the ocean for a number of years. They run 110 to 120 miles an hour and he won more than his share of races. Now that's crazy.

He is also an expert with guns and "sites" them for hunters from three or four states. But what Bright does best is cook and he can cook for the masses. By that I mean 1,200 people at one time or 3,000 on a weekend. He helped cater the first Wild Life Expedition in Charleston and he taught his younger brother Jimmy Stevenson all he knows.

Steamed Oysters
BRIGHT STEVENSON

Best steamer pot available. Bright built his.
A bushel of very fresh oysters. He gets his from
Apalachicola, Fl.

*Build a very hot fire under the steamer. Fill steamer
with water. When water comes to a boil put the oysters in a basket above the water and close the lid. He
gets his water 35 or 40 degrees hot.*

   *Allow to steam until they first start to open. The
time you see the first one open a little bit take them
out and they are ready to eat.*

Bright's Cocktail Sauce

1 bottle of catsup
Horseradish, a little
Wine vinegar, a little
Black pepper and salt, to taste
Garlic, a little
Red wine
Lemon juice, a little

*Mix all together and serve with oysters and saltine
crackers*

Barbecured Shrimp
CATHY & GERALD SEASE

48 large shrimp peeled and deveined (about 3 lbs.)
2 teaspoons oregano
1 cup water
1 to 2 teaspoons ground
½ cup sliced green onions
red pepper flakes
½ cup cane syrup
½ teaspoon salt
2 tablespoons butter or stick margarine
½ teaspoon pepper
1 teaspoon hot sauce
6 cloves garlic, minced
1 tablespoon Worcestershire sauce
2 bay leaves
2 teaspoons paprika
cooking spray
2 teaspoons dried thyme
12 inch Skewers
Optional: Bacon

CONTINUED

Peel shrimp; reserve shells; cover and chill. Combine shells and water in saucepan and bring to boil. Reduce heat and simmer 10 minutes. Strain in large bowl; discard shells.

Combine broth, onions and next 12 ingredients (onions thru bay leavers) in large saucepan; bring to boil; reduce and simmer 10 min. Cool at room temperature. Combine shrimp and syrup mixture. Cover and marinate in refrigerator 1 hr.

Prepare grill. Remove shrimp from dish; reserve marinade. Place marinade in small saucepan and bring to boil. Cook 1 min. and remove from heat.

Thread 6 shrimp onto 12" skewers. Place kebabs on grill rack coated with cooking spray and grill for 6 minutes. Serve with reserved marinade if desired.

Kicked up: To marinade, add bacon sliced long enough to wrap around shrimp. Wrap shrimp with bacon, thread onto skewers and then grill.

Shrimp & Dumplings
PAPPY POSTON

1 stick butter or margarine
1 medium white or red onion sliced
½ stalk celery sliced crosswise
1½ qt. chicken stock
2 tbs. white flour
2 to 24 oz. pkgs. Frozen dumplings (Ann's)
1½ lbs. small uncooked shrimp (headed & peeled)
1 to 10 oz. can uncooked chopped okra drained
   (fresh or frozen equivalent)
1 to 10 oz. can whole baby clams, drained
½ cup water

Slowly heat chicken broth in pot on low heat. Melt butter or margarine in skillet. Sauté onion and celery in the butter until soft, but not brown. Stir into chicken broth. Simmer for 15 minutes. Add dumplings, one at a time, stirring broth into each. When dumplings are done, add clams. Stir in okra. Mix water and flour into paste and stir into broth mixture. When broth begins to thicken, add shrimp a little at a time. Cook until shrimp are pink. Serve in bowls.

JIMMY SWAN

A native of Florida, Jimmy lives in West Palm Beach. He shuns Miami, Florida State and Florida as they are too close to home. He adopted the Gamecocks as his favorite team in 1999 when the Cocks went 0-11. Since then he has not missed a game at home or away.

Jimmy loves to read and drive. Give him a book on cassette and an open road and he is in heaven. An excellent driver he is blissful when Carolina is playing in Baton Rouge, Tennessee or Arkansas.

He logs about 50,000 miles a year on his car and is looking forward to Carolina playing Oregon State or Southern Cal.

Jimmy is the best customer of the Okeechobee Steak House and that is where he got this recipe.

Okeechobee Steak House Shrimp Scampi Sauce

JIMMY SWANN

5 lbs. Land of Lakes Butter, melted
1 pint white wine
3 spoonfuls of salt
1 pint jar chop garlic
1 pint dry chives
2 spoonfuls dry yellow mustard
½ pint tarragon vinegar
2 small bottles of Lea and Perrin's

Whip butter, white wine, Lea & Perrin sauce, tarragon vinegar. Whip all together until they become thick. Then add the rest. Then freeze. Boil shrimp.

College Shrimp

ZOE & ALEX SANDERS
FROM HER BOOK
"ENTERTAINING AT COLLEGE OF CHARLESTON"

3 lbs. large shrimp, peeled, deveined and dried
⅔ cup olive oil
2 sticks of butter
1 Tbl. Cavender's Greek Seasoning
Two (13 x 9 x 2) oven-proof glass baking dishes

Preheat oven to 400 degrees.

Divide oil and butter between baking dishes and heat in 400 oven until butter is melted and just beginning to turn brown.

Divide shrimp between baking dishes and stir until covered with oil and butter. Sprinkle Cavender's Seasoning over shrimp. Bake at 400 degrees for 6 minutes, or until shrimp turns pink and curls. Do Not Overcook. Stir again and serve.

Serve College Shrimp over hot white rice and add some of the buttery juices to give rice a good flavor.

Crab Imperial

TOM PRICE

Lump back fin crabmeat is expensive and hard to find, but Sam's Club stores usually have it in one pound cups at a reasonable price. Although intended as a main dish crab imperial is ideal at tailgating and similar parties spread on crackers or served as a dip.

¼ cup butter, melted and divided (4 tablespoons)
1 green onion, minced (I sometimes use two or
  three if they are small)
2 tablespoons flour
⅛ teaspoon ground red pepper
⅛ teaspoon white pepper
⅛ teaspoon ground mace
½ cup milk
½ cup Half & Half (I sometimes use one cup milk &
  eliminate the H & H if I'm cholesterol conscious)
2 to 3 tablespoons dry sherry
½ cup mayonnaise
Juice of one lemon
Salt to taste

CONTINUED

1 pound lump crab meat
Paprika for garnish

Combine 2 tablespoons butter and onion in a heavy saucepan over medium heat; stir until lightly browned, 5 to 8 minutes. I find 5 minutes is usually enough.

Stir in flour, peppers and mace for 1 to 2 minutes. Add milk, cream and sherry. Cook until thick and smooth, about 3 to 4 minutes, to create a roux or sauce.

Remove from heat. Stir in mayonnaise, lemon juice and salt. Set aside.

Combine remaining 2 tablespoons butter and crab in a large, heavy skillet over medium heat. Cook 1 minute and fold sauce into crab. Sometimes I add about a quarter pound of cooked shrimp as a variation, creating Crab/Shrimp Imperial, a dish no one else had ever heard of.

Spoon mixture into Corning Wear or other baking dish. May be prepared in advance to this point and refrigerated until time to bake. Sprinkle with paprika to add color.

Bake at 350 degrees for 12 to 15 minutes or 20 to 25 minutes if prepared in advance.
Servings: 4 servings as a main dish or more if spread on crackers as an appetizer or hors d'oeuvre.

Devil Crab

JIM GUEST

Jim got this recipe from Doris Cook, when the Edisto Restaurant was open in Jacksonboro.

1 cup onions, chopped
¼ cup green pepper
4 tablespoons butter

2 tablespoons flour
1 cup milk
1 pound crab meat
4 hard boiled eggs, grated
Salt and pepper to taste
1 tablespoons mustard
1 tablespoon lemon juice
2 tablespoons Worcestershire sauce
Butter
Paprika

Sauté onions and peppers in butter and flour until soft. Add milk gradually and cook, stirring constantly, until thickened. Add to crabmeat with grated eggs, salt, pepper, mustard, lemon juice and Worcestershire sauce. Put in crab shells. Top with bread crumbs. Dot with butter. Sprinkle with paprika on top. Brown under broiler.

These can be frozen.

Marinated Srimp Medley

SUSIE & HEYWARD KING

2 lbs. medium shrimp, shelled and cooked
1 can artichoke hearts
1 can ripe olives
1 can mushroom caps
1 or 2 cups cherry tomatoes
(Use more or less of the ingredients you like best)

Mix all of the above; pour Italian dressing over and chill for several hours or overnight.

PHIL PETTY

Quarterbacks generally get too much credit when they win and too much blame when they lose. Such was the case of Phil Petty.

In 1999 he quarterbacked the Gamecock's to a 0-11 season. The last time Carolina had a winless season was in 1897.

In 2000 Phil quarterbacked the Gamecocks to an 8-4 season. The following year he improved that with a 9-3 record. Phil is the only QB in the history of the school to win back to back Bowl games, and his 17-7 two year record is the best in 110 years of Gamecock football.

Shrimp and Grits
PHIL PETTY

2 cups water
1 (14 oz.) can chicken broth
¾ teaspoon salt
¾ cup half and half
¾ teaspoon salt
1 cup regular grits
¾ cup shredded Cheddar cheese
¼ cup grated Parmesan cheese
2 tablespoons butter
¼ teaspoon hot sauce
¼ teaspoon white pepper
3 bacon slices
1 pound medium-size shrimp, peeled and deveined
¼ teaspoon black pepper
⅛ teaspoon salt
¼ cup all-purpose flour
1 cup sliced mushrooms
½ cup low-sodium, fat free chicken broth

2 tablespoons fresh lemon juice
¼ teaspoon hot sauce
Lemon wedges

Bring first 4 ingredients to a boil in a medium saucepan; gradually whisk in grits. Reduce heat, and simmer, stirring occasionally, 10 minutes or until thickened. Add cheddar cheese and next 4 ingredients. Keep warm

Cook bacon in a large skillet until crisp; remove bacon, and drain on paper towels, reserving 1 tablespoon drippings in skillet. Crumble bacon, and set aside.

Sprinkle shrimp with pepper and salt; dredge in flour.

Sauté mushrooms in hot drippings in skillet 5 minutes or until tender. Add green onions and sauté 2 minutes. Add shrimp and garlic, and sauté 2 minutes or until shrimp are lightly brown. Stir in chicken broth, lemon juice, and hot sauce, and cook 2 more minutes, stirring to loosen particles from bottom of skillet.

Serve shrimp mixture over hot cheese grits. Top with crumbled bacon. Serve with lemon wedges

Smoked Salmon Rolls & Horseradish Cream

BECKY & RICK WALLACE

2 oz thinly sliced smoked salmon
2 tablespoons Horseradish cream
1 tablespoon capers
1 teaspoon chopped fresh dill

HORSERADISH CREAM
⅓ cup heavy cream
12 teaspoons Dijon mustard
1½ tablespoons drained horseradish
1 tablespoon sour cream
salt and pepper to taste

HORSERADISH CREAM
Blend the cream and mustard in a food processor or in a bowl with an electric mixer until the mixture forms soft peaks, about 1 minute. Whisk together the horseradish, sour cream, salt and pepper until smooth. Fold the mustard cream mixture into horse-radish mixture. Serve immediately or store in a air-tight container in the refrigerator for up to 5 days

ROLLS
Cut the salmon into 1 inch strips. Put a small dollop of horseradish cream on one end of the salmon strip and top with a caper and sprinkle of dill. Roll up the salmon strips, jelly-roll style. And secure with tooth-picks. Serve immediately.

Soft Shell Crab

SCOTT KYLE

Scott is my son and a great cook. ~Charlie

Soft shell crabs
1 cup, all purpose flour
½ teaspoon baking powder
Salt and pepper
Peanut Oil

Put about 1½ inch of peanut oil in frying pan. Get real hot. Mix flour, baking powder, salt and pepper. Cover crabs, shake off excess.

Fry 2 or 3 minutes on each side.

Make sure the soft shell crabs have been cleaned.

I also cooked this using clarified butter. It was a much richer taste.

DESSERTS

Best-Ever Rum Cake ~ Sam Rigby & Boon Threat

Pound Cake ~ Dot & Stanhope Spears

Pound Cake ~ Harold Green

Chocolate Chip Pound Cake ~ Jim & Orrland Moss

Four layer Chocolate Delight ~ Ria & Edwin Floyd

Chocolate Cake ~ Becky & Lem Harper

Million Dollar pie ~ Ed Pitts

Lemon Square ~ Dot & Stanhope Spears

Lemon Meltaways ~ Cathy & Gerald Sease

Sweet Dreams Cookies ~ Julie & John Saunders

Brownies ~ Betty & Don Barton

Banana Pudding ~ Stephanie & Bobby Bryant

Sand Tarts ~ Gwen Adams

Pistachio Salad Dessert ~ Jackie & Mackie Prickett

Congo Squares ~ Susie & Heyward King

Brown Sugar Pound Cake w/ carmel frosting ~ Linda Flowers

Banana Pudding ~ Miriam & Johnnie Vereen

Better Than Sex Cake ~ Janice Marthers

Rice Krispie Scotcharoos ~ Lisa and Shawn Bishop

Grandma Ida Maie's Apple Dapple Cake ~ "Big Daddy" Howard Hughes

Pistachio Cake ~ Joyde Pooser

Ice Box Pudding ~ John Frierson

Liz's Boosy Bourbon Balls ~ Eddie Elmore

Pecan Pie ~ Lisa

Martha's Marvelous Brownies ~ Weemie Baskin

Monkey Bread ~ Caitlyn Murdaugh

Red Velvet Cake ~ Jenny & Governor Mark Sanford

Red Velvet Cake ~ Donna Parker

Cobbler ~ Cathy Huggins

Homemade Banana Pudding ~ Coach Kristi Coggins

Chocolate Delight ~ R.J. Moore

Date Nut Bars ~ Ruth Harmon

Deep Dish Apple Pie ~ Phil Petty

Cold Oven Pound Cake ~ Donna Parker

Chocolate Pound Cake ~ Margaret Price

Lemony Buttermilk Pie ~ Stuart Whatley

Sour Cream Crunch Cake ~ Jake Bodkin

Sherry Cake ~ Gwen Miller

Banana Split Pie ~ Cathy Murdaugh

Patsy Chocolate Cake ~ Charile Hawkins

SAM RIGBY & BOONE THREAT

Boone can cook and drink. Sam can do never....well or alone.

Best-Ever Rum Cake

SAM RIGBY & BOONE THREAT

1 teaspoon sugar
1 cup dried fruit
1 teaspoon baking soda
2 large eggs
1 or 2 quarts of rum
Brown sugar
1 cup butter
Baking powder
Nuts

Before starting, sample run to check quality. Good, isn't it? Now, proceed. Select large mixing bowl, measuring cup, etc. Check rum again. It must be just right.

To be sure rum is of the best quality, pour one level cup of rum into a glass and drink it as fast as you can. REPEAT.

With electric mixer, beat 1 cup of butter in a large fluffy bowl. Add 1 seaspoon of thugar and beat again. Meanwhile, make sure rum is still alright. Try another cup. Open second quart if necessary. Add leggs, 2 cups fried druit, and beat until high. If druit gets stock in beaters, pry loose with a drewscriver. Sample rum again, checking for toncsistricity. Next suft 3 cyos oeooer ir sakt (ut reakkt diesb't matter which). Sample rum. Sift ½ pint lemon juice. Fold in chopped butter and strained nuts. Add 1 bablespoon of brown sugar or whatever color you can find. Mix well.

Grease oven. Turn cake to 350 gedrees. Pour mess into boven and ake. Check rum again and – bo to ged.

Pound Cake

DOT & STANHOPES SPEARS

BLEND
1 stick of butter
½ cup Crisco
2¼ cups sugar
Add 5 eggs, 1 at a time
Add 3 cups flour,
1 cup milk
2 teaspoons vanilla (starts with flour and end with flour)
Add last ½ teaspoon baking powder

Put into a greased-flour dusted tube cake pan.

Put in COLD oven and bake at 350 degrees for 1 hour and 10 minutes. DO NOT OPEN OVEN DOOR. Test with tooth pick.

My Grandmother's Pound Cake

HAROLD GREEN

1 lb. butter, at room temperature
2 cups sugar
6 eggs, at room temperature
3 cups all-purpose flour
3 teaspoon baking powder
1 cup evaporated milk, approx.
2 teaspoons lemon or vanilla extract

Preheat oven to 350 degrees. Grease and flour a Bundt pan or two 9 x 5 inch loaf pans. In a large bowl, beat butter until creamy; gradually add sugar and continue to beat until fluffy. Add eggs one at a time, beating after each addition. Sift together flour and baking powder; add to butter and sugar, 1 cup at a time, beating after each addition. Add milk as required, up to 1 cup. Blend in extract. This batter will be thick; it cannot be poured—spoon it into prepared pan and bake or until cake tester comes out clean.

Chocolate Chip Pound Cake

ORRAL ANNE & JIM MOSS

1 pkg. yellow cake mix (one that doesn't say moist)
1 pkg. instant chocolate pudding mix (reg. size)
4 eggs
¾ cups water
1 stick unsalted butter, melted
1 pkg. chocolate chips
Powdered sugar

Beat eggs with water. Add mix (cake) and pudding mix. Slowly add melted butter. Stir in chocolate chips. Stir as little as possible. Do Not Use Mixer or all your chips will end up on the bottom. Bake in greased and floured tube or bunt pan at 325 degrees for about 50 minutes or until done. Stick a straw (broom) in cake; if it comes out clean, it's ready. Cool only a short while and then turn out and sift powdered sugar over top.

Four Layer Chocolate Delight

RIA & EDWIN FLOYD

FIRST LAYER
2 sticks butter
2 cups self-rising flour
1 cup pecans, chopped

Mix well and pat on bottom of 9 x 12 inch pan. Bake at 350 for 20 minutes until brown.

SECOND LAYER
12 oz. cream cheese
1 cup powdered sugar
2 cup cool whip

Blend with beater and spread over cooled crust.

THIRD LAYER
2 small packages instant chocolate pudding
3 cups milk
Whip until thick and pour over second layer

FOURTH LAYER

Cover top with additional cool whip and grate Hershey Chocolate bars to spread evenly over top.

Oh So Moist Chocolate Cake
BECKY & LEM HARPER

4 tablespoons cocoa
2 sticks margarine
1 cup water
2 cups sugar
2 cups all-purpose flour
½ cups buttermilk
2 eggs, slightly beaten
1 teaspoon vanilla
1 teaspoon soda

Bring to boil the water, margarine and cocoa. Measure sugar and flour in large bowl. Pour boiled mixture over this and stir until smooth. Add buttermilk, eggs, vanilla and soda. Bake in a well greased and floured 11 x 16 inch loaf pan at 400 degrees for 20 minutes. While still hot spread on icing.

5 minutes before cake is done:

ICING
In pot bring to a rapid boil:

4 tablespoon cocoa
1 stick margarine
6 tablespoons milk

Remove from heat and add:
1 box 10xxxx sugar
1 cup nuts, chopped
1 teaspoon vanilla

Spread on cake while both are still hot.
   Servings: This will make 60 to 65 brownie size squares

ED PITTS

Ed was a two-way tackle for the Gamecocks from 1957-1959. He made some All American teams and All Atlantic Coast Conferences. He co-captained the 1959 team with fullback John Saunders

Million Dollar Pie
ED PITTS

1 graham cracker pie crust
1 container of cool whip
1 small can of Eagle Brand Condensed Milk
½ cup of lemon juice

Mix ingredients together and pour into graham cracker pie crust. Freeze for 45 minutes and then keep refrigerated.

Lemon Squares
STANHOPES AND DOT SPEARS

BOTTOM LAYER
½ cup butter
1 cup sifted Swan Down Cake flour
¼ cup confection sugar

Mix, put in 9 x 9 pan.
Bake 15 minutes at 350 degrees.

TOP LAYER
1 cup sugar
½ teaspoon baking powder
3 tablespoons fresh lemon juice & some of pulp
2 tablespoons Swans Down Cake flour

¼ teaspoon salt
2 eggs beaten

Mix all ingredients and pour over base. Bake 25 minutes at 350 degrees.

Sift confection sugar lightly over top.

Lemon Meltaways

CATHY & GERALD SEASE

COOKIES
1¼ cups all-purpose flour
½ cup cornstarch
⅓ cup powdered sugar
¾ cup butter, softened
1 teaspoon grated lemon rind
1 teaspoon lemon juice

FROSTING
¾ cup powdered sugar
¼ cup butter, softened
1 teaspoon grated lemon peel
1 tablespoon lemon juice

In large mixer bowl, combine all cookie ingredients. Beat at low speed, scraping bowl often until well mixed (2 to 3 minutes). Divide dough in half. Shape each half into 8 x 1 inch roll. Wrap in plastic food wrap. Refrigerate until firm (1 to 2 hrs).

Heat oven to 350 degrees. With sharp knife, cut each half into ¼ inch slices. Place 2 inches apart on cookie sheets. Bake 8 to 12 minutes or until set (cookies will not brown unless overcooked!) Cool completely.

In small mixer bowl combine all frosting ingredients. Beat at medium speed, scraping bowl often until fluffy (1 to 2 minutes). Frost cooled cookies.

JOHN SAUNDERS

In 1958 John won the Jacobs Blocking Trophy for both the state of South Carolina and the ACC. He made all ACC and led the conference in rushing.

Injuries side lined him for most of the 1959 season and more or less eliminated any chance for a pro football career. John chose instead to sell hammers and nails and turned it into a very lucrative living.

Sweet Dream Cookies

JULIE & JOHN SAUNDERS

1 cup unsalted butter
1½ cup Light brown sugar
1 egg room temperature
1 teaspoon vanilla
2 cups flour
1 teaspoon baking soda
1 teaspoon cinnamon
1 teaspoon ground ginger
½ teaspoon salt
1 12 oz. pkg. chocolate chips
1 cup chopped walnuts
Powdered sugar

Cream butter and beat in sugar, egg, and vanilla. Combine flour, baking soda, spices and salt and add to butter. Mix. Refrigerate at least 1 hr. (can be left overnight) Roll into balls then roll in powdered sugar and place on lightly greased cookie sheets. Bake in preheated over 375 degrees for 10 minutes. Cool on sheet 5 minutes.

Brownies

BETTY BARTON

3½ squares chocolate
1 box brown sugar
¾ cups white sugar
2 sticks margarine
4 eggs
1½ cups flour
1 teaspoon vanilla
1 to 2 cups nuts, chopped

Melt, chocolate, 2 sugars and margarine over medium heat. Remove from heat. Beat eggs, one at a time. Mix all together. Grease 15 x 12 x 1 inch pan Cook 350 degrees for 30 minutes.

BOBBY BRYANT

In my mind and in many others Bobby Bryant is the best athlete to ever attend the University of South Carolina. An All American defensive back in 1966, his 98 punt return is still a school record.

Drafted by the New York Yankees and the Boston Red Socks he was the first pitcher at USC to strike out 100 batters in a single season. He won the McKevlin Award in 1966-67 as the top athlete in the ACC.

His 14 years as a starting cornerback for the Minnesota Viking is unheard of. His 50 career interceptions was a Vickings team record. Bobby has played in four Super Bowls and is, of course, in the state and school's Hall of Fame.

Bobby Bryant's Famous Banana Pudding

STEPHANIE & BOBBY BRYANT

1½ boxes vanilla wafers
2 12 oz. cans evaporated milk
5 or 6 good sized bananas
3 eggs, separated
Beat yolks and add to sauce (below) before it gets
   warm, otherwise it will curdle)

SAUCE
2 cups evaporated milk
3 egg yolks, beaten
2 cups sugar
1 tablespoon vanilla flavoring

Heat slowly, but do not bring to fast boil, stirring it to keep from sticking, until it thickens.

In the bowl you are going to serve it in (3 qt. size), place a layer of vanilla wafers at the bottom, then a layer of sliced bananas, then another layer of wafers, alternating until almost to the top of the bowl.

Pour the thickened sauce over the top of all the layers of wafers and bananas. Beat the remaining 3 egg whites until stiff, and then add to the top of the pudding. Place bowl in oven, and broil for about 2 minutes, to lightly brown the whites.

Refrigerate for several hours before serving.

Sand Tarts

GWEN ADAMS

½ cup Crisco
1 cup sugar
1 egg
1½ cups plain flour
½ teaspoon baking powder
½ teaspoon salt
1 teaspoon vanilla

Blend Crisco, sugar. Add egg and remaining ingredients. Roll and cut. Bake at 350 degrees for 12 minutes (until brown on bottom).

FOOL PROOF ICING
1 stick oleo
3 squares chocolate

Melt the above and blend.

1 lb. powdered sugar
1 egg beaten
½ teaspoon vanilla

Stir into melted chocolate butter. Spread onto cookies.

Pistachio Salad or Dessert
JACKIE & MACKIE PRICKETT

1¾ oz. package Pistachio Instant Jello-Pudding
2 8 oz. Cool Whip
1½ cups of small marshmallows
1 can crushed pineapple with the juice (can size 1 lb. 4 oz.)

Mix all together in large bowl or container—let it set until marshmallows soak up all the cool whip. Cover and put in refrigerator. Serve in small dishes or cups.

Congo Squares
SUSIE & HEYWARD KING

1½ sticks of butter, melted
1 box light brown sugar
3 eggs
1 teaspoon vanilla
2½ cups self-rising flour
1 cup nuts, chopped
1 cup semi-sweet chocolate chips

Mix butter and sugar. Add eggs, one at a time. Beat until smooth. Add vanilla, and add flour slowly. Beat well. Stir in nuts and chocolate chips.
Bake in greased and floured 9 x 13 inch pan for 25 to 30 minutes at 350 degrees.
Do Not Overbake.

Brown Sugar Pound Cake
LINDA FLOWERS

1 box golden brown sugar
1 cup granulated sugar
3 sticks butter, softened
5 eggs
3 cups all-purpose flour
½ tsp. salt
1 tsp. vanilla
1 tsp. baking powder
1 tsp. maple flavoring
1 cup milk
1 cup chopped nuts (optional)

Cream sugars and butter well. Add eggs, 1 at a time, beating well after each. Mix flour, salt and baking powder together. Add flavorings to milk. Add flour and milk mixture alternately to batter, starting and ending with flour and beating just to blend. Add nuts. Put in greased and floured 10 inch tube pan. Bake at 350 degrees for 1 hour to 1¼ hours, or until toothpick comes out clean.
Cool before frosting. Caramel frosting followers:

CARAMEL FROSTING
1 stick butter
1 cup brown sugar, firmly packed
¼ cup milk
3 cups sifted confectioners' sugar

Melt butter in saucepan; add brown sugar. Boil over low heat, stirring constantly. Add milk and, still stirring constantly, bring to a boil again. Remove from heat, beat 4 minutes. Add the sifted confectioners' sugar and beat until spreading consistency. May add milk if too thick. Ices one 1—inch tube pan cake or 2 layer 8-inch cake, or one 13 x 9 sheet cake.

Banana Pudding

MIRIAM & JOHNNIE VEREEN

50 to 60 vanilla wafers
6 medium size fully ripe bananas
1¼ cup sugar
⅔ cup flour
¼ tsp. salt
6 eggs (room temperature)
2¼ cups milk
⅔ tsp. vanilla extract
2 tablespoon butter

In double boiler (or sauce pan) combine sugar, flour and salt over medium heat. Slowly add milk. Bring to boil. Add egg yolks, stirring constantly until thickened (about 5 minutes) Remove from heat and add vanilla and butter. Spread small amount on bottom of 2 qt. casserole and cover with layer of vanilla wafers. Top with layer of sliced bananas. Pour about ⅓ of custard over bananas. Continue to layer wafers, bananas and custard to make 3 layers of each-ending with custard.

MERINGUE
½ cup sugar
6 egg whites (room temperature)
½ tsp. cream of tartar
½ tsp. vanilla flavoring

Beat egg whites until stiff but not dry, gradually add sugar and cream of tartar. Beat until stiff peaks form. Add vanilla flavoring. Spoon on top of pudding being sure to seal edges. Bake at 350 or until golden brown.

Better Than Sex Cake

JANICE MARTHERS

1 box of cake mix
½ cup of water
½ cup of oil
3 eggs
1 box of instant pudding
2 Hershey's candy bars, grated
½ bag of chocolate chips
8 oz. sour cream

Grease and flour cake or bundt pan. Bake for 1 hour at 350 degrees.

Rice Krispie Scotcharoos

LISA AND SHAWN BISHOP

6 cups Rice Krispies
1 cup peanut butter
1 cup light karo syrup
1 cup sugar
1 pkg. semisweet chocolate morsels
1 pkg. butterscotch morsels

In large saucepan combine Karo syrup and sugar and stir over low heat until sugar is melted. Remove from burner and stir in peanut butter. Then stir in Rice Krispies and press mixture into 13 x 9 inch pan. Melt chocolate and butterscotch morsels together and stir. Spread over Rice Krispie mixture and cool.
Cut into small squares—Very sweet!

greased and floured tube pan. Bake for 45 minutes to 1 hour at 350 degrees (no peeking until at least 45 minutes). Remove cake from pan into lipped plate.

Spoon frosting over entire surface of hot cake, allowing it to run down and around the sides.

Jodye's Pistachio Cake
JODYE & BERT POOSER

1 box Duncan Hines White Moist Cake Mix
½ cup Wesson Oil
½ cup warm water
½ cup Breakstone sour cream (no lite) or pet sour cream
5 eggs
2 boxes Jell-O Pistachio pudding

Preheat oven to 325 degrees. Cake: Combine cake mix, oil, water, sour cream and pudding mix. Blend well together and beat about four minutes at medium speed. Add one egg at a time and mix well. Do Not Overbeat!

Pour into three round layer cake pans or a 9 x 13 x 2 inch pan. Be sure to grease and flour pans. I usually also line with wax paper.

Cook at 325 degrees for 25 minutes or until lightly brown (if using cake pans). Cook sheet pan 35 minutes or longer.

ICING
1 box powdered sugar
1 stick butter, room temperature
1 box Pistachio pudding
Sour Cream

Mix and beat well on high the pudding and butter.

Grandma Ida Maie's Apple Dapple Cake
HOWARD HUGHES

1½ cups oil
3 eggs
3 cups unsifted all-purpose flour
1 teaspoon salt
1 cup of peeled, chopped raw apples (Washington State preferred)
2 cups sugar
2 teaspoon vanilla
1 teaspoon baking soda
1½ cups chopped pecans

FROSTING
1 cup light brown sugar (packed)
1 stick margarine (use butter if you dare)

Mix oil, sugar, eggs, and vanilla. Add flour, baking soda, salt, chopped pecans, and apples. Pour into

Add enough sour cream for consistency to spread on cake layers. Be sure not to add too much sour cream or it may be too runny. I usually add a little sour cream at time to get the consistency I need. You must beat well on high so pudding mix will not be grainy in icing and in order to get smoothness.

Ice Box Pudding
JOHN FRIERSON

Here is the best desert I have ever had the privilege to enjoy. It was made by my Grandmother, Nora Minnick Bowman (Mrs. V.E. Bowman) of the Green Springs community near Abingdon, Va: Notice that the recipe is not cooked due to the fact it was made during the Civil war.

½ cup cocoa
1 cup confectionary sugar
1 teaspoon hot water
3 egg yolks
3 egg whites
1 teaspoon vanilla

Mix together sugar, cocoa, add hot water and egg yolks—mix well, fold in egg whites.

1 cup confectionary sugar
½ cup butter
3 egg yolks
3 egg whites, stiffly beaten
1 cup coconut

Cream together butter and sugar, add egg yolks and coconut—fold in egg whites, then pour in bottom of pan which has been covered with crushed vanilla wafers. Cover with layer of vanilla wafer crumbs. Then pour in 1st part and cover with vanilla wafer crumbs. Chill overnight and serve next day with vanilla ice cream on top. "Yum yum."

THEO EDWARD ELMORE JR.

Who was a dedicated gamecock alumnus. I was lucky enough to be born his senior year at Carolina.

Liz's Boosy Bourbon Balls
EDDIE ELMORE

This recipe is in memory of my father.

1 6oz package of semisweet chocolate chips
½ cup granulated sugar
3 Tabs light corn syrup
½ cup bourbon

CONTINUED

2½ cups finely crushed vanilla wafers
1 cup finely chopped nuts
2 cups sifted power sugar

Melt the chocolate chips in top of double boiler set over simmering water. Stir constantly until chocolate is melted. Remove from heat and stir in sugar and corn syrup. Add bourbon and blend well. Combine vanilla wafers and chopped in a large bowl. Add the chocolate mixture to the wafers and nuts; mix well. Form the mixture in to 1inch balls. Roll the balls into powder sugar. Place the balls in a airtight container and let set for several days before serving.

Pecan Pie

LISA

½ (15 oz.) package refrigerated piecrust
4 large eggs
1 cup light corn syrup
¾ cup sugar
⅓ cup butter or margarine, melted

Pinch of salt
1 teaspoon vanilla extract
1 cup chopped pecans
¾ cup pecan halves

Fit piecrust into a 9" pie plate according to package directions; fold edges under, and crimp. Bake piecrust for about 10 minutes at 350 degrees until slightly browned.

Beat eggs and next 5 ingredients at medium speed with an electric mixer until smooth. Stir in chopped pecans; pour into prepared piecrust. Arrange pecan halves on top.

Bake at 350 degrees for 50 minutes, shielding edges with aluminum foil after 30 minutes to prevent excessive browning.

LITTLE WEEMIE BASKIN

Don't look in the record books because he's not there, but he probably should be. Little Weemie was a starting receiver for the Gamecocks from 1956-1958, but he never caught a pass. Not one. He did, however, intercept a pass, against Miami in 1956.

Weemie will always be remembered for the touchdown pass he dropped in the Maryland game in 1958 that kept us out of the Orange Bowl.

To a man, none of his team mates will ever forgive him and none of us have spoken to him since.

This is the only good picture we could fine of Weemie

Martha's Marvelous Brownies

WEEMIE BASKIN

2 sticks margarine
1 cup of water
4 heaping tablespoons baking cocoa
2 cups sugar
2 cups flour
2 eggs
½ cup buttermilk (tsp. soda in buttermilk)
Sprinkle of salt,
1 teaspoon vanilla

Melt margarine in large pot, add water and cocoa. Let bubble. Take off heat.

Add sugar, flour, eggs, and ½ cup buttermilk (tsp. soda in buttermilk). Mix, and add salt, and vanilla.

Bake at 400 degrees for 15 minutes.

ICING

½ stick butter
3 heaping tablespoons cocoa
⅓ cup milk
1 box powdered sugar
1 teaspoon vanilla

In saucepan add butter, cocoa and milk. Let bubble. Sir in powdered sugar and vanilla.

Monkey Bread

CAITLYN MURDAUGH

1 cup of margarine or butter
⅓ cup granulated sugar
⅓ cup brown sugar
1 cup finely chopped nuts
1 tablespoon cinnamon
3 cans of buttermilk biscuits

Preheat oven at 375. Prepare bundt pan with cooking spray or butter; set aside.

Melt margarine or butter (not diet) in a bowl. In another bowl mix sugar, brown sugar, nuts, and cinnamon.

Open one can of biscuits, separate. Cut each biscuit into 4 sections and roll into a ball. Put each ball into sugar mixture, coat well; and then drop into bundt pan. After finishing first can of biscuits drizzle a little butter evenly over top. Repeat this step with other 2 cans of biscuits.

Sprinkle remaining sugar mixture over the top and bake for 30 to 35 minutes.

When done remove from oven and let cool for a minute or two, turn onto a plate and remove from pan. If you leave monkey bread in bundt pan much longer, it will stick and is very hard to remove.

Red Velvet Cake
GOVERNOR & MS. JENNY SANFORD

Vegetable oil for the pans
1½ cups all-purpose flour
1½ cups sugar
1 teaspoon baking soda
1 teaspoon fine salt
1 teaspoon cocoa powder
1½ cups vegetable oil
1 cup buttermilk, at room temperature
2 large eggs, at room temperature
2 tablespoons red food coloring (1 oz.)
1 teaspoon white distilled vinegar

1 teaspoon vanilla extract
Cream Cheese frosting, recipe follows
Crushed pecans, for garnish
Preheat the oven to 350 degrees. Lightly oil and
  flour 3 (9by 1½ inch round) cake pans.

In a large bowl, sift together the flour, sugar, baking soda, salt and cocoa powder. In another large bowl, whisk together the oil, buttermilk, eggs, food coloring, vinegar, and vanilla.

Using a standing mixer, mix the dry ingredients into the wet ingredients until just combined and smooth batter is formed.

Divide the cake batter evenly among the prepared cake pans. Place the pans in the oven evenly spaced apart. Bake, rotating the pans halfway through the cooking, until the cake pulls away from the side of the pans, and a toothpick inserted in the center of the cakes comes out clean, about 30 minutes.

Remove the cakes from the oven and run a knife round the edges to loosen them from the sides of the pans. One at a time, invert the cakes onto a plate and then 43-invert them onto a cooling rack, rounded sides up. Let cool completely.

Frost the cake. Place 1 layer, rounded-side down, in the middle of a rotating cake stand. Using a palette knife or offset spatula spread some of the cream cheese frosting over the top of the cake. (Spread enough frosting to make a ¼ to ½ inch layer.) Carefully set another layer on top, rounded-side down, and repeat. Top with the remaining layer and cover the entire cake with the remaining frosting. Sprinkle the top with the pecans.

CREAM CHEESE FROSTING
1 lb. cream cheese, softened
4 cups sifted confectioners' sugar
2 sticks unsalted butter (1 cup), softened
1 teaspoon vanilla extract

In a standing mixer fitted with the paddle attachment, or with a hand-held electric mixer in a large bowl, mix the cream cheese, sugar, and butter on low speed until incorporated. Increase the speed to high and mix until light and fluffy, about 5 minutes. (Occasionally turn the mixer off, and scrape down the sides of the bowl with a rubber spatula.

Reduce the speed of the mixer to low. Add the vanilla, raise the speed to high and mix briefly until fluffy (scrape down the bowl occasionally). Store in the refrigerator until somewhat stiff, before using. May be stored in the refrigerator for 3 days.

Yield: enough to frost a 3 layer (9-inch) cake

Red Velvet Cake
DONNA PARKER

2½ cups cake flour – sifted
1½ cups sugar
1 teaspoon cocoa
1 teaspoon baking soda
2 eggs
1½ cup Crisco oil
1 teaspoon vinegar
1 teaspoon vanilla extract
1 cup buttermilk
1 small bottle red food coloring
*NOTE: Mix soda and flour together, then sift.

Mix sugar and cocoa together. Add eggs, one at a time. Add oil. Then flour and buttermilk. Add vinegar and vanilla. Add food coloring last. Bake at 350 degrees for 30 minutes. Makes three layers

ICING
1 stick margarine
1 8 oz. cream cheese
1 teaspoon vanilla
1 box powdered sugar
1½ cup chopped pecans
Milk—enough to make spreadable

Mix the above. Spread between layers and on cake

Cobbler
CATHY HUGGINS

1 cup Bisquick
1 cup sugar
4 cups fruit
1 Tablespoon lemon juice
1 stick butter
1 egg

Preheat oven to 375 degrees.

Mix Bisquick and sugar together. Put fruit in baking dish. Pour lemon juice over fruit. Pour melted butter over fruit.

Beat egg and mix with Bisquick and sugar. Mix until lumpy
Sprinkle over fruit.

Bake at 375 degrees for 35 or 40 minutes.

Homemade Banana Pudding

COACH KRISTI COGGINS
WOMEN'S GOLF HEAD COACH

2 boxes of Vanilla Wafers
6 bananas sliced into ¼ inch slices
1½ cup white sugar
¼ cup all-purpose flour
2 cups milk
3 egg yolks
2 teaspoons butter
2 teaspoons vanilla extract
1¼ cup white sugar

Preheat oven to 350 degrees.
Line bottom and sides of a 9 inch pie plate with a layer of vanilla wafers with a layer of sliced bananas on top.

TO MAKE PUDDING

In a medium saucepan, combine 1½ cups sugar with flour. Mix well, then stir in half the milk. Beat egg yolks and whisk into sugar mixture. Add remaining milk and butter.
   Place mixture over low heat and cook until thickened, stirring
frequently. Remove from heat and stir in vanilla extract. Pour half of the pudding over vanilla wafer banana layer while still hot. Make another layer of wafers and bananas and pour remaining pudding on top of second layer.

TO MAKE MERINGUE

In a large glass or metal bowl, beat egg whites until foamy. Gradually add ¼ cup sugar, continuing to beat until whites are stiff.
   Spread meringue over pudding in pie pan making sure completely covering pudding layer.
   Bake in preheated oven for 15 minutes, just until meringue is browned. Chill before serving.

Chocolate Delight

R. J. MOORE
COURTESY OF JUDY JONES

CRUST
1¼ sticks margarine
1¼ cups flour
½ or ¾ cups chopped pecans

Mix and spread in a 12½ x 8 Handi Foil pan. Bake until medium to dark brown. Cool—Take a potato masher and break crust.

FIRST LAYER
1½ 8 oz. cream cheese
1¼ cup 4 x sugar
8 to 10 oz. cool whip

Mix and spread on top of crust.

SECOND LAYER
1 small chocolate Instant pudding and pie filling
1 large vanilla instant pudding and pie filling
5 cups skim milk

Mix, Spread over first layer

THIRD LAYER
Rest of cool whip (about 8 or 10 oz.)

Sprinkle with finely chopped pecans.

Serve: About 20 to 25 people

Date Nut Bars

RUTH HARMON

1 small pkg. dates
1 cup nuts
1 cup plain flour
1 teaspoon baking powder
¼ teaspoon salt
1 cup sugar
3 eggs

Cut up dates and nuts. Sift dry ingredients add dates and nuts and mix. Beat eggs in a cup with a spoon and add to other ingredients and mix with spoon. This will seem dry, but will soon become moist. Then I use 2 square cake pans and grease and flour these. Then half the mixture in the pans. It will look like it won't fill the pan, but it will spread when it starts cooking. Cook at 350 degrees for 15 to 20 minutes. I test with a straw at 15 minutes. Sift powdered sugar on top and cut in squares.

Deep-Dish Apple Pie

PHIL PETTY

12 cups tart cooking apples
1½ cups granulated sugar
½ cup all-purpose flour
1 teaspoon ground cinnamon
1 teaspoon nutmeg
¼ teaspoon salt
Pastry for 9-inch single crust pie
2 tablespoon butter

Heat oven to 425 degrees. In large bowl, combine apples (8-10 Granny Smith or similar-peeled, cored and thinly sliced). Sugar, flour, cinnamon, nutmeg (preferably freshly grated) and salt. Toss together to mix well. Spoon into 9-inch baking pan. Dot over top with butter. Place pastry crust over top; make some slits near center. Fold edges under and crimp. Bake 1 hour, or until juice begins to bubble through slits in crust and apples are tender.

Serve warm with or without ice cream

Cold Oven Pound Cake

DONNA PARKER

2 sticks margarine
½ cup Crisco
2½ cup sugar (Dixie Crystals)
5 eggs
3 cups cake flour-sifted
½ teaspoon baking powder
1 cup milk
1 tablespoon vanilla extract
1 tablespoon lemon extract

Cream margarine and Crisco together. Add sugar, a little bit at a time. Add eggs, one at a time, and mix well after each one. Add flour and milk, then lemon and vanilla extracts. Add baking powder last.

Bake at 325 degrees for 1½ hours or until done. DO NOT PRE-HEAT YOUR OVEN!!!

Miss Leila's Chocolate Pound Cake
AS PREPARED BY MARGARET PRICE

Cream together two sticks (one half pound) of butter, one half cup Crisco and three cups sugar.

Add five eggs one at a time. Mix thoroughly.

Stir together three cups all-purpose flour, one half-cup cocoa, one half-teaspoon baking powder, one-fourth teaspoon salt.

Add flour mixture to creamed mixture alternating with milk (one cup plus two tablespoons).

Add one-teaspoon vanilla flavoring.

Bake in tube pan (greased and floured) at 300 degrees for one hour and fifteen minutes.

Stuart's Lemony Buttermilk Pie
STUART WHATLEY

½ cup all-purpose flour
1½ cup sugar
Pinch of salt
3 eggs
½ cup buttermilk (Whole)
1 stick (8 tbls.) unsalted butter, melted
½ cup fresh lemon juice
2 teaspoons lemon extract
1 teaspoon vanilla extract

Beat eggs until frothy. Add melted butter—Makes sure it's cool. Add lemon juice, vanilla, lemon extract, buttermilk. Combine. Add sifted flour, sugar and pinch of salt, Combine.

Add ingredients to partially cooked pie crust. Bake at (preheated) 350 degrees for 35 minutes. Let cool and then chill in fridge for at least 2 hours Put berry mixture on top.

TOPPING
½ pint fresh blueberries—I tried fresh blackberries
Juice of ½ a lemon
3 tablespoons sugar

Combine. Stir, let sit in fridge for at least 1 hour (overnight is better for blueberries), stirring occasionally—Blackberries have more juice and seem to break down much quicker than blueberries. I guess the acid from the lemon juice accelerates the breakdown.

Sour Cream Crunch Cake
JAKE BODKIN
COURTESY OF CHARLIE HAWKINS

2 sticks butter
3 cups sugar
3 cups flour
¼ teaspoons soda
6 eggs

1 cup sour cream
Cinnamon
Nuts, pecans

Cream butter, add sour cream, and then sugar ½ cup at a time. Alternate eggs and additions of ½ cup flour, finishing with egg, beating well after each. Put half of batter in greased tube pan and sprinkle lightly with cinnamon and ½ cup chopped nuts. Cover with remaining batter and cover top with ½ cup nuts and cinnamon. Cook at 300 degrees for 1½ hours. Remove and cover with another pan for 15 minutes before removing cake from pan.

GLAZE
1 cup sugar
1 stick margarine
¼ cup of water
¼ cup of Sherry

Mix all of the above together pour batter into a greased tubed pan and bake at 350 degrees for 45 minutes. While cake is baking prepare the glaze. For the glaze boil the mixture for a few minutes over medium heat. When the cake is done pour ⅓ of the glaze over the cake immediately. Wait a few minutes and pour ⅓ more then wait about 15 more minutes. Turn cake out of pan and pour the rest . This is prepared on Thursday before the game.

Touchdown Sherry Cake
GWEN MILLER

1 box of Duncan Hines yellow butter cake mix
1 small box vanilla pudding mix (not instant)
¾ cup of Gallo Sherry (do not use cream sherry)
4 eggs

Banana Split Pie
CATHY MURDAUGH

1 cup margarine
1 box confectioner's sugar
2 eggs
2 graham cracker piecrusts
5 bananas
1 large can of drained crushed pineapple
1 large cool whip
Pecan pie

Combine first three ingredients and beat for 15 minutes. Spread filling on top of two graham cracker piecrusts. Slice 5 bananas (dividing) over this. Then sprinkle 1 large can drained crushed pineapple over this. Top with 1 large cool whip. Garnish with pecans. Refrigerate.

Patsy's Chocolate Cake

CHARLIE HAWKINS

2 sticks butter
3 tablespoons cocoa
1 cup water

Bring to boil and pour over flour mixture. Mix together well.

2 cups cake flour
2 cups sugar
½ teaspoon salt

Mix together and add to the other mixture.

2 eggs, beaten
1 teaspoon soda
½ cup buttermilk
1 teaspoon vanilla

Mix well. Pour all into pan (11" x 15" x 1").
Bake for 30 minutes at 375 degrees. Make icing while cake bakes the last 5 minutes.

1 stick butter
3 tablespoons cocoa
6 tablespoons milk
1 Box 4 x sugar
½ cup pecans, (I like them toasted)
1 tablespoons vanilla

Melt butter, cocoa and milk in pan. Mix other ingredients and put on cake as fast as it comes from oven.

CHARLIE'S BEST COLLECTIONS

As I have previously mentioned Charlie is an exceptionally gifted cook. By gifted, I mean she was blessed with an acute sense of taste and smell. She can tell when I've been drinking by the time I get to the mailbox, and the mailbox is one half a mile from the house.

About ten years ago I was in Tuscaloosa, Al. with a friend who said he was taking me to the best Bar B Que house in the country. Dreamland was the name of the place and they had been in business since 1958. It was situated in a residential neighborhood and served only barbeque ribs and two pieces of white bread. That's it...Ribs and white bread.

Well I knew it had to be good to stay in business for that length of time with a menu that limited. And it was.

Upon leaving I bought a quart of their patented Bar B. Que sauce to take home with me. The sauce consisted of basically ten ingredients.

I bet my friend $20.00 that Charlie could taste it once and tell us seven of the ten ingredients. He took the bet.

Upon entering the house I put a small amount of this sauce on Charlie's finger and she named all of the ten ingredients with no hesitation. I won the $20.00.

I had done the same experiment on Charlie with McCabe's barbeque sauce the year before.

The following are some of her original recipes and others with some modification. Pay close attention to her seasoning as that is what sets her apart.

Artichoke Dip

1 cup mayonnaise
1 cup parmesan cheese
¼ teaspoon garlic powder
1 cans (14 oz.) artichoke hearts, drained and finely chopped.

Butter shallow dish. Combine all and bake at 350 degrees for 15 or 20 minutes. Use as a dip or spread. This taste like oysters

Fighting Gamecock Dip

1 tablespoon butter
1 small red bell pepper, chopped
1 small green bell pepper, chopped
1 medium onion, chopped
2 15 oz. cans black beans, drained
2 teaspoons fresh chopped jalapeno chilies
½ teaspoon ground cumin
1 cup salsa (I like the kind in the cooler section)
16 oz. Sharp cheddar or Co-Jack cheese, shredded
1 container (12 oz. refrigerated guacamole
2 cups shredded lettuce
½ cup sour cream

Melt butter in skillet; add peppers and onion. Cook over medium heat, stirring occasionally, until onion is softened. Stir in beans, jalapeno chilies and cumin. Continue cooking until heated through.

Transfer 1 cup bean mixture to food processor. Cover, process on high speed; until smooth. Return blended mixture to remaining bean mixture; stir to combine. Spread been mixture into 11 x 8 inch (2 qt.) baking dish. Cover; refrigerate 2 hours or overnight.

Just before serving, evenly layer salsa, cheese, guacamole and shredded lettuce over bean mixture.

Spread sour cream into resealable plastic food bag. Snip off corner. Pipe sour cream over lettuce to resemble yard lines on football field.

Servings: Serve with tortillas chips Serves 15

I sometimes add ½ pound of lean ground round, cooked and drained.

Florentine Tomatoes

4 firm ripe tomatoes
1 package (10 oz.) frozen chopped spinach
2 tablespoon oil or butter
3 green onions, chopped
½ teaspoon dill weed
¼ teaspoon pepper
½ cup crumbled Feta cheese
4 tablespoon sour cream

Cut a thin slice off top of tomatoes. Gently squeeze out seeds. Scoop out pulp. Chop. Sprinkle with salt. Drain on rack.

Cook spinach until thawed. Press out liquid Sauté green onions in oil. Add spinach, tomato pulp, dill and pepper. Cook until most of liquid is absorbed, about 5 minutes.

Stir in cheese and sour cream. Fill tomato shells. Place in oiled baking dish.

Bake at 375 degrees for 20 minutes. Serve

Servings: 4

Polish Sausage in Sauce

5 pounds Polish sausage (Hillshire Farms)
1 onion
1 16 ounces sour cream
5 teaspoons mustard
2 teaspoons paprika
1 teaspoon garlic powder
1 teaspoon Tony Ca spice
1 cup red wine

Cook sausage in a little olive oil. Remove sausage. Sauté onions in gravy Add wine, and all the other ingredients.

Serve this in a crock pot at very low temperature.

Cavier Log

1 – 4¾ oz. can liver pate
1 – 2 oz. jar black caviar
4 – 3 oz. package cream cheese

Have pate caviar and cream cheese at room temperature.

Place cream cheese in waxed paper. Use the paper to roll and shape cheese into a log.

Spread evenly with liver pate, carefully cover with caviar. Lightly cover with clear plastic wrap; Chill for 1 hour. Serve with Melba toast rounds.

Serves: 1 Log

Charlie's Devil Eggs

12 boiled eggs
1 medium onion, finely chopped
3 or 4 tablespoons Duke Mayonnaise
1 teaspoon French's mustard
½ teaspoon Lawry's Seasoning Salt
½ teaspoon Tone's Garlic and Herbs
½ teaspoon Ms. Dash

Put eggs in cold water to cover and bring to a boil. Turn stove off and cover. Let sit about an hour.
Peel under running water. Cut in half, long ways. Mash yolks really good. Add the onions, mayo and mustard. Add the seasoning. (You may want to adjust it more to your liking). Put mixture in white half.

Garnish with paprika and pickled jalapeño slices.

Caesar Salad

I got this recipe in 1960 in Dallas, Texas

2 cloves garlic
1 tablespoon wine vinegar
2 tablespoon lemon juice
1 glass fine white wine
1 egg (coddled) 3 minutes
½ teaspoon anchovy paste
⅓ cup olive oil
½ cup seasoned croutons
½ medium size head of Romaine lettuce
⅓ cup Parmesan cheese, grated (This has to be fresh)

Break garlic in large salad bowl. Add vinegar and lemon juice. Let soak for hour or so. Drink the glass of wine. Remove garlic from liquid and rub sides of

CONTINUED

bowl. *Dice half of one clove and leave in liquid. Add coddled egg, olive oil and anchovy paste. Tear Romaine into bite size pieces and toss with croutons and sprinkle with Parmesan cheese.*

SEASONED CROUTONS
French bread (stale) cut in small squares

In sauce pan put a stick of butter, garlic powder with Herbs, Ms. Dash and fresh parsley. Let melt and combine. Pour over bread on a cookie sheet.
  Cook 250 degrees, 15 minutes or until brown.
  Grate parmesan cheese over and put in airtight bag.

Warm Goat Cheese Salad

This was a 1997 Recipe Hall of Fame

  ½ cup olive oil
  ⅓ cup lemon juice
  1 tablespoon diced green onions
  1½ teaspoons Dijon mustard
  1/2 cup Italian-seasoned breadcrumbs
  1½ tablespoons grated Parmesan cheese
  1½ tablespoons sesame seeds
  3 (4 oz.) goat cheese logs
  1 large egg, lightly beaten
  3 tablespoons butter or margarine
  6 cups torn mixed salad greens
  12 pitted ripe olives, sliced

Combine first 4 ingredients; set aside.
  Combine breadcrumbs, parmesan cheese, and sesame seeds.
  Cut each goat cheese log into 4 slices. Dip in egg, and dredge in breadcrumb mixture. Cover and chill for

2 hours. Melt butter in a large skillet over medium-high heat. Add goat cheese, and fry 1 to 2 minutes on each side or until browned; drain on paper towels.*
  Toss mixed greens with dressing; add olives, and top with warm goat cheese.
Servings: 6

Orange Congealed Salad

  1 package orange or lime jello
  1 cup chopped nuts
  1 small can crushed pineapple
  3 ounces cream cheese, soft
  ¾ cup Pet milk
  ½ cup mayonnaise

Mix jello, cream cheese and mayonnaise with hot water and stir. Add milk, pineapple and nuts

Pink Salad

This can be used as a dessert.

Put in saucepan and bring to boil:

  2 tablespoons sugar
  1 teaspoon flour
  ½ cup water

Add while hot:

  1 package strawberry Jell-O
  ½ package marshmallows (18) cut up
  1 large can carnation milk
Cool and add:

  1 small cup crushed pineapple

1 banana
½ jar cherries, cut up
Juice of 1 orange (optional)
1 large tablespoon mayonnaise

Blue Mama Spinach Casserole

2 packages frozen spinach, chopped
1 package Lipton's dried onion soup
1 cup Pepperidge Farm crumbs, mixed with a
   tablespoon of melted butter
½ pint sour cream (2-8oz)

Boil spinach. Mix sour cream and onion soup and let stand ½ hour. Add to spinach with ¾ bread crumbs.

Bake in greased dish at 375 degrees for 30 minutes.
Add rest of crumbs on top.

I often put oysters in this and it taste like Oysters Rockefeller.

Pineapple Casserole

1 cup sugar
6 tablespoons all-purpose flour
2 cups grated sharp cheddar cheese
2 (20-ounce) cans pineapple chunks, drained, and
6 table. pineapple juice reserved
1 cup cracker crumbs (I use Ritz)
1 stick butter, melted, plus extra for greasing pan

Preheat the oven to 350 degrees.
Grease a medium- size casserole dish with butter.
In a large bowl, stir together the sugar and flour.

Gradually stir in the cheese. Add the drained pineapple chunks, and stir until ingredients are well combined. Pour the mixture into the prepared casserole dish.

In another medium bowl, combine the cracker crumbs, melted butter, and reserved pineapple juice, stirring with a rubber spatula until evenly blended. Spread crumb mixture on top of pineapple mixture.

Pan Fried Tomatoes

This is a very old recipe. Author unknown

½ cup all-purpose flour
¼ cup white cornmeal
1 teaspoon salt
6 large green tomatoes
¼ cup peanut oil
3 tablespoons butter
Black pepper to taste

Combine four, cornmeal and salt. Wash and core the tomatoes. Slice about ¼ inches thick, discarding end pieces. Coat each slice with flour and cornmeal mix, Heat oil with the butter over medium heat. Fry the prepared slices in the hot oil, using a spatula carefully to turn each slice. When brown on both sides, sprinkle very lightly with pepper and serve immediately.

Sometimes I put the tomato slices in ice water for a few minutes. Make sure to dry completely before putting flour and cornmeal on.

Cabbage Casserole

I got this recipe from a friend in Fair Play, S.C. many years ago.

1 head of cabbage, cut in bite sizes
2 cans cream of celery soup
1 package sharp cheddar cheese
Corn flakes
1 stick butter
¼ cup mayonnaise
¼ cup milk

Crush corn flakes. Melt butter and mix. Use as a pie crust. Add cabbage next.

Mix soup with mayo and milk and put on top of cabbage. Top it off with whole corn flake and cheese. Cook at 350 degrees and 30 minutes.

Green Beans and Tomatoes

2 cans whole green beans, drained
2 cans whole tomatoes
4 pieces of bacon
2 tablespoons of flour
1 teaspoon of garlic powder, or as much as you like
1 bell pepper
1 small onion, chopped

Fry bacon until partly crisp. Remove. In grease add onions and pepper; flour and garlic. Cook until brown. Add vegetables and bacon. Mix well with salt and pepper. Put in long glass dish. Bake until bubbly hot at 350 degrees.

Creamy Fresh Corn

6 to 8 ears fresh white corn
3 strips bacon, halved
⅔ cups water
1 teaspoon salt
¼ cup milk
⅛ teaspoon pepper
1 tablespoon butter

Husk corn and cut kernels from cob. Scrape cob, for milk. Cook bacon until crisp in a 8" skillet. Remove and drain. Stir corn into hot bacon grease. Let cook for a few minutes. Add water, salt and a little tiny bit of sugar. Cook and stir 8 minutes uncovered. Add milk and stir constantly a few minutes until thickened. (If it does not thicken, add a little cornstarch mixed with water to thicken). Add the pepper and butter. Serve hot. Garnish with bacon.

Deviled Asparagus

You really need to double this.

1 medium can cut asparagus
½ box cheese Ritz crackers
1 tablespoon green bell pepper
1 teaspoon Worcestershire sauce
1 tablespoon chopped pimento
1 can cream of mushroom soup
½ stick butter, or margarine
1 tablespoon onion juice
½ teaspoon Tabasco sauce

Mix all seasoning with soup. Put layer of soup in casserole and add drained asparagus. Top with crackers that have been buttered. Top this with sliced almonds.

Heat at 350 degrees for about 30 minutes or so.

Spinach with Cream

Alex loves this dish and I know you will also.

4 bunches of fresh spinach, washed and dried.
   (Make sure you wash them good)
2 cups white sauce
⅓ cup grated Gruyere cheese
Butter, salt, pepper and paprika.

Place spinach in boiling salted water and add some pepper. Cook 3 minutes. Cool spinach and drain and squeeze leaves, chop. Butter baking dish and add chopped spinach. Dab with a bit of butter. Season with salt, pepper, and paprika. Pour white sauce over spinach and sprinkle with cheese. Broil 10 minutes in oven. Serve Hot.

WHITE SAUCE
Heat 4 tablespoons butter in saucepan. When hot mix in 4 tablespoons of flour and cook one minute over medium heat. Incorporate half of (2½ cups hot milk) with whisk. Add remaining milk, a pinch of nutmeg, salt and pepper; stir well. Bring sauce to boil. Cook 10 to 12 minutes over low heat. Stir several times.
Serves: 4

Carrot Casserole

This came from my 96 years old aunt, who got it from her aunt's 91 years old cook 40 years ago. Makes you wonder how old this recipe is.

1 pound carrots
½ cup butter
1 cup sugar
3 eggs
1 tablespoon all purpose flour
1 teaspoon baking powder
1 teaspoon vanilla

Cook carrots in a little salt until tender. Combine butter and carrots in blender and blend well. Put in greased 1 quart casserole dish.

Cook 45 minutes at 350 degrees.

Tomato Supreme

6 medium tomatoes sliced
1 small onion, thinly sliced
1 cup seasoned croutons
¼ cup grated Parmesan cheese
1½ teaspoons basil
1 teaspoon pepper
3 tablespoons butter

Layer tomatoes, onions and croutons in shallow buttered casserole dish. Sprinkle with cheese, basil and seasonings. Dot with butter.

Bake uncovered at 350 degrees at 30 minutes.

I make my own croutons from butter, parmesan cheese and onions, much better than bought ones.

Baked Vidalia Onion

4 medium large Vidalia onions
4 beef bouillon cubes
4 tablespoons butter
Salt and pepper to taste

Hollow out a small area in the top of each onion. Place onions in a glass baking dish. Put one bouillon cube and 1 tablespoon butter into hollow. Season. Cover with silver paper for oven. Saran wrap for microwave and cook on high for 10 to 12 minutes. In oven about 45 minutes at 350 degrees.

Optional, grated cheese, cracker crumbs, parsley, or fresh herbs.

Roasted New Potatoes

2 to 3 pounds of new white, or red potatoes
6 tablespoons butter
3 tablespoons olive oil
3 cloves garlic, finely chopped
½ cup parsley, chopped
1 tablespoon fresh thyme or ½ teaspoon dried thyme
1½ teaspoons rosemary
1½ teaspoons paprika
Cayenne pepper to taste
Ms. Dash and Lawry's seasoning salt to taste

Preheat oven to 375 degrees. Clean potatoes and pat dry. Potatoes may be sliced or cooked whole. In a roasting pan, melt butter in oil. Add all spices except Ms. Dash and Lawry's salt. Add the potatoes, mixing them well so that they are coated with mixture. Bake for about 40 minutes or until potatoes are tender,

basting occasionally. Season with Ms. Dash and Lawry's if needed.
Servings: 10 servings

Spanish Spaghetti

1½ lb. lean ground beef
1 medium onion
2 teaspoon salt
1 can tomatoes (28oz.)
¾ small bottle of catsup
1 can mushrooms
1 green bell pepper
1 (8oz.) package spaghetti

Brown meat and onions in heavy pan. Add salt (Do not stir after meat and onions are brown). Break up spaghetti and spread over meat. Pour tomatoes, soup, chopped green pepper, catsup and mushrooms over spaghetti. DO NOT STIR. Cover and bring to a full boil, turn heat down to simmer for 1 hour. DO NOT REMOVE LID. When ready to serve mix well.

I cook this in a crock pot. When Miss Mary cooked, we didn't have electric crackpots.

Sicilian Meat Roll

2 beaten eggs
¾ cup soft bread crumbs (1 slice)
½ cup tomato juice
2 tablespoons snipped parsley
½ teaspoon dried oregano, crushed
¼ teaspoon each, salt and pepper
1 close garlic, minced

2 pounds lean ground beef
8 thin slices boiled ham
6 oz. mozzarella cheese, shredded (1½ cups)
3 slices mozzarella cheese, halved diagonally

Combine eggs, crumbs, juice, parsley, oregano, salt, and pepper and garlic. Add beef; mix well. On waxed paper or foil, pat meat to a 12 x 10 inch rectangle. Arrange ham atop meat, leaving a small margin around edges. Sprinkle shredded cheese over ham-starting from short end, carefully roll up meat, using paper to lift; seal edges and ends. Place roll, seam side down in 13 x 9 x 2 inch baking pan. Bake at 350 degrees till done 1¼ hrs. (Center of roll will be pink due to ham) Place cheese wedges over top of roll and return to oven until cheese melts, about 5 minutes.
Serves: 7

Meat Loaf

This is Alex's favorite.

1 lb. ground beef
1/2 ground veal
1/2 lb. ground pork
1 medium onion, finely chopped
2 1/2 cup soft bread crumbs
2 eggs
1½ teaspoon salt
Freshly ground blk. Pepper
2½ teaspoons fresh thyme leaves or 1½ teaspoons dried
½ teaspoon Italian seasonings
6 slices of bacon
1 small can tomato sauce

Preheat oven 350 degrees.

In large bowl combine the meats with the onion, thyme, bread crumbs, eggs, salt and pepper and mix well with a fork. Form the mixture into loaf.

Line the bottom and up sides of a baking dish with pieces of bacon. Lay meat loaf on top of bacon. Cover top with bacon. (the bacon adds flavor & keeps loaf moist.)

Bake about 1 hour.

Cover with tomato sauce (Alex eats his without tomato sauce).

TOMATO SAUCE FOR MEATLOAF

After meat loaf is cooked drain juice into skillet from meat loaf.

2 cups canned Italian Plum tomatoes
1 clove of garlic (don't let garlic burn)
3 tablespoons olive oil
2 tablespoons butter

Bring to a boil the above, reduce heat and simmer until sauced is thick. 30 or 35 minutes. Add salt and pepper and1/4 cup chopped fresh parsley. Taste. If sauce is a little acid add more butter and simmer a little longer.
Serves: 4 to 6

Chicken Roll Ups

My niece Edie Edwards Smith gave me this wonderful recipe. This is good to take to tailgating. Just cook it after you get there.

1 cup molasses
½ teaspoon ginger
¼ teaspoon garlic powder
2 tablespoons Worcestershire

CONTINUED

¼ cup soy sauce
¼ cup olive oil
¼ cup lemon juice
12 boneless chicken breast—pound to ½ inch
   thickness. Marinate chicken for 8 hours.

STUFFING
Sauté 2 lbs. mushrooms
20 green onions
½ cup margarine
½ teaspoon spicy seasoning

Take chicken out of marinade, but save the marinade.
   Place chicken on shallow pan.
   Place small amount of stuffing on chicken. Roll chicken up and tie with piece of bacon.
   Grill on charcoal grill for 1 hour.
   Baste with marinade every 15 minutes.

Charlie's Low Fat Chicken

2 tablespoons Land of Lake low fat butter
3 chicken breast
¼ cup no fat chicken broth
1 tablespoon parsley, fresh
1 lemon
Ms. Dash, your taste
Lowry's seasoning salt, your taste

Heat over to 350 degrees
   Heat butter in iron fry pan, medium heat. Add chicken and brown three minutes. Turn and season. Cook 3 more minutes. Put in oven 20 minutes. Remove chicken from pan and put iron pan over high heat on top of stove and add juice of lemon and cook 1 minute. Add chicken broth and parsley. Cook 2 minutes. Check

your seasoning. Pour sauce over chicken.
   Even lower fat, remove chicken skin before serving. But cook with skin on.

Brunswick Stew

Whole chicken (4-6 lb.) chopped
1½ lbs. coarsely ground chuck
1 lb. coarsely ground lean pork
1 large onion, chopped
1 large bottle of catsup
1 (#3) cans tomatoes, mashed
2 (#3) cans yellow corn, cream style
1 (17 oz.) whole kernel sweet corn
1 tsp. ground red pepper
2 small lemons and a little Worcestershire sauce

Cook chicken and pull from bone. Put aside. Cook beef, pork and onions in 2 cups of chicken broth. (make sure meat is covered with broth) Cook very slowly for 1 hour. Salt and pepper. Add catsup, tomatoes and cook another hour. (be sure and stir so it won't stick), Add corn, chicken and red pepper, Ms. Dash and Worcestershire. Cook slowly for 1 hour. Stir often. Use a heavy pot to cook this and do not put a lid on top after vegetables are added. This gets better each time you warm it up. I usually freeze some in small containers for later.

Black, Crusty Gamecock Pork Roast

1 (2or 3 lb.) pork roast
1 (8oz.) jar French's yellow mustard
1 large onion, thinly sliced
1 tablespoon vinegar

Preheat oven to 275 degrees. Place roast in large dish. Cover top and sides of roast with mustard. Next cover with sliced onions. Add 1 inch of water to bottom of pan. Add vinegar. Bake at least 6 hours at 275 degrees.

   Roast will become black, crusty and delicious.

Beef Brisket

Beef brisket with lots of fat on bottom or it will be tough.

   Put brisket in silver paper and add pepper, garlic powder, brown sugar and a package of Lipton's Onion Soup in order. Cook fat side up. Just enough water to cover sides of meat. Cover with silver paper and cook 2½ to 3 hours at 350 degrees.

   I usually use 3½ to 4½ lb. meat. (cover well)

Charlie's Spaghetti

2 lbs. ground round
4 medium onions, chopped
1 green bell pepper
6 cloves garlic, chopped
2 big cans of Italian tomatoes with basil, cut up

2 small cans of tomato sauce
2 small cans of imported tomato paste
1 small can of mushrooms
1 can sliced water chestnuts, cut up once again
½ cup olive oil
3 bay leaves, crushed
2 tablespoons Worcestershire sauce
Ms. Dash
Lawry's seasoning salt
Dash of Tabasco sauce
Parmesan cheese, grated (fresh)

In a large skillet sauté meat, adding seasoning salt and Ms. Dash in ½ cup of olive oil. In another pan, use remaining olive oil and sauté onions, garlic and bell pepper until transparent. Put all together, adding tomato sauce and paste, mushrooms, bay leaves and chestnuts. Add Worcestershire and Tabasco. Stirring constantly until sauce comes to full boil. Reduce heat to very low and simmer several hours.

   I sometimes add green and black olives, cut up to the sauce.

   Cook spaghetti, drain and put butter in and mix well.

   Spoon sauce over spaghetti and grate some fresh parmesan cheese over top.

Servings: 6 to 8

Chicken Marsala

2 tablespoons unsalted butter
1 tablespoon vegetable oil
4 boneless skinless chicken breast halves
4 slices mozzarella cheese
(1 ounce each)
12 capers, drained
4 flat anchovy fillets, drained

CONTINUED

1 tablespoon chopped fresh parsley
1 clove garlic, minced
3 tablespoons marsala wine
⅔ cup heavy or whipping cream
Hot cooked pasty (optional)

Heat butter and oil in large skillet over medium-high heat until melted and bubbly. Add chicken; reduce heat to medium. Cook, uncovered, 5 or 6 minutes per side until chicken is tender and golden brown. Remove chicken with slotted spatula to work surface. Top each chicken piece with 1 cheese slice, 3 capers and 1 anchovy fillet.

Return chicken to skillet. Sprinkle with parsley. Cover and cook over low heat 3 minutes or until cheese is semi melted and juices from chicken run clear. Remove chicken with slotted spatula to heated serving platter; keep warm.

Add garlic to drippings remaining in skillet; cook and stir over medium heat 30 seconds. Stir in marsala; cook and stir 45 seconds, scraping up any brown bits in skillet.

Stir in cream. Cook and stir 3 minutes or until sauce thickens slightly. Stir in salt and pepper. Spoon sauce over chicken. Serve with pasta.

Garnish with sage leaves or whatever.

Veal Piccata

4 tablespoons butter
2 tablespoons oil
1 pound veal, thinly sliced
Flour to coat veal
¼ cup dry white wine
2 tablespoons lemon juice
2 tablespoons parsley, chopped

Lemon slices
Parsley springs
1 tablespoon capers

Heat 2 tablespoons of butter and oil in skillet over medium heat. Dredge both sides of veal in flour and shake off excess. Cook veal until lightly browned on each side. Place on platter and keep warm. Season with Ms. Dash and Lawry's salt. Over low heat, add wine to skillet drippings, scraping up brown bits with wooden spoon. Cook until wine begins to evaporate. Add lemon juice, remaining butter, and parsley. Return veal to skillet and turn to warm and coat with sauce. Remove to platter and garnish with lemon slices and parsley.

Suggestion: California Gamay Beaujolais.
Servings: 4 to 6

Herb-Crusted Pork Tenderloins

1 pork tenderloin (1-2 lb.)
1 teaspoons Lawry's seasoning salt
1 teaspoon Ms. Dash
¾ teaspoons garlic herb seasoning
1 tablespoon olive oil (extra virgin)
¼ cup chopped fresh parsley
1 teaspoon dried thyme
2 cloves garlic, finely chopped
½ teaspoons Herbs of Provence
½ teaspoons chives
Sprinkle of Pepperidge Farm Herb Seasoned stuffing
Parsley or Thyme sprigs for garnish

Heat oven to 425 degrees. Rub pork with Lawry's and Ms. Dash. Heat 1 teaspoon olive oil in large nonstick skillet over high heat. Add pork, brown on both sides about 5 minutes.

Meanwhile combine parsley, thyme, garlic and Herbs of Provence and chives. Add about 2 teaspoons olive oil in small bowl. Rub or brush all over pork. Place in small pan lined with Reynolds wrap.

Roast in 425 degrees over about 15 minutes. DON"T OVER COOK.

Let stand 5 minutes. (It continues to cook after taken out of oven). Slice diagonally, ¼ inch thick. Add a little water to pan dripping to make more gravy.

Veal Vermouth

2 pounds of veal cutlets
Flour
2 teaspoons bacon grease
½ cup butter
¼ cup onions, diced
½ cup Vermouth
½ pound mushrooms, chopped
2 green peppers, chopped
2 large ripe tomatoes, chopped
1 clove garlic, diced
½ cup ham, finely diced

Pound the cutlets thin and sprinkle with flour on both sides. Place olive oil, bacon grease and butter in skillet. Add onion and sauté. Add veal and brown slowly about five minutes on each side. Add Vermouth, cover and simmer for five minutes. Add chopped mushrooms, green peppers and tomatoes. Cover and simmer 5 more minutes. Add diced garlic and ham and simmer, uncovered for 10 minutes until done. (If it gets dry too fast add more Vermouth.) I have used chicken broth instead of Vermouth, and it is still good.
Servings: 4 to 6

Beef Willington Fillets

8 to 5 fillets of beef
1 lb. ground beef sirloin
1 clove garlic, crushed
1 tablespoon snipped parsley
8 frozen patty shells, thawed
1 slightly beaten egg white
Golden Tarragon Sauce

Place fillets in freezer for 20 minutes. Brush with oil; sprinkle with Lawry's and fresh ground pepper. In hot skillet brown the fillets for 4 minutes on each side. Refrigerate. Combine ground beef, garlic, parsley, ½ teaspoon salt and pepper.

Divide mixture into 8 portions; place a rounded portion atop each fillet. Refrigerate.

Roll each patty shell to a 9 x 5 rectangle, ⅛ inch thick. Place fillet, sirloin side down on each rectangle. Fold over one side of pastry then other end, then other side and finally other end; seal. Place seam side down in shallow baking pan.

Top with cut out from an additional rolled out patty shell if desired.

Before serving, brush pastry with beaten egg whites. Bake at 450 degrees for 10 minutes for rare, 12 minutes for medium rare and 15 for medium.

Serve with Golden Tarragon Sauce.

GOLDEN TARRAGON SAUCE
3 egg yolks
½ cup butter, melted
2 tablespoons lemon juice
2 tablespoon hot water
¼ teaspoon salt
1 teaspoon snipped parsley
⅛ teaspoon dried tarragon, crushed

CONTINUED

Beat egg yolks in top of double boiler with wire whisk until smooth, but not fluffy. Add butter, lemon juice, hot water and salt. Place over hot not boiling water; beat till sauce begins to thicken, about 5 minutes. Stir in parsley and tarragon. (If mixture begins to separate add a small about of cold water and beat).
Makes about ¾ cup.

Charlie's Chili

Package of ground venison
1½ lb. ground round
1 bell pepper, I mix it with red, yellow and green
1 medium onion
Tablespoon bacon grease
3 cloves garlic
3 tablespoons Ms. Dash
4 tablespoons Lawry's Seasoning salt
1 package McCormick Chili seasoning
1 can RoTel tomatoes, Mexican Festival
2 cans whole peeled tomatoes.
1 small can mushrooms, pieces
1 can sliced water chestnuts, break them up
1 tablespoon Worcestershire sauce
1 tablespoon red pepper flakes
3 teaspoons Cumin
2 dashes of dry mustard

Brown meats in bacon grease with bell pepper, onion, garlic. Add seasoning. Add Rotel and whole tomatoes. Take the stem out of the tomatoes and break up into small pieces. Add all the juices. If need add about cup of chicken broth.
Cook for about an hour covered on simmer.
Add dry mustard, and cumin and the red pepper flakes.

Chili powder. I use several dashes, I like it spicy. Add water chestnuts, broken up and chili beans. Turn off and let sit for a while. It gets better as it ages.
To serve: Put in bowls and top with chopped onions, grated strong cheddar cheese, sour cream and jalapeños.

Oyster Rockafeller

1 package frozen Spinach
¼ cup butter melted
¼ cup bread crumbs
2 Tablespoons grated onions
Salt and pepper to taste
Worcestershire to taste
Tabasco to taste
1 tablespoon lemon juice
1 tablespoon parsley, minced
12 oysters
Additional bread crumbs
Parmesan cheese, grated

Cook spinach and drain well. Add next 8 ingredients. Spread on Oysters.
Sprinkle with additional bread crumbs and parmesan. Place in oven and bake at 400 degrees about 5 minutes or until edges of oysters begin to curl.
I put in individual shells.

Hot Peppered Shrimp

1 lb. butter
½ cup finely chopped onion
1 tablespoon paprika
1 tablespoon black pepper
1 tablespoon bitters
1 tablespoon garlic powder
2 tablespoons Lawry's Seasoned salt
1 tablespoon Worcestershire sauce
2 tablespoons wine vinegar
Shrimp, medium size

In a bowl beat butter until light, add remaining ingredients, except shrimp. Beat until well blended. Store butter mix in refrigerator and use as needed.

Peel and devein raw shrimp. Heat 3 tablespoons of mixture in frying pan. When it starts to bubble stir in 8 to 10 shrimp. Stir quickly for 1 or 2 minutes, until shrimp are just cooked. Pour into bowl with its juices and serve with Cobblestone rolls. I dip bread in sauce.

Grouper with Parmesan Cheese and Lemon Butter

This is my favorite fish recipe. Chef Philip Bardin, The Old Post Office, Edisto Island, gave to me.

Grouper (nice thickness)
Japanese bread crumbs
Fresh Parmesan cheese
Lemon butter
Garlic

Grate cheese and mix with equal amount of bread crums and a couple or so garlic closes, minced. Put on top of grouper. Put in refrigerator for 30 mimutes. Cook at 500 degrees about 15 minutes. Cool. Put lemon butter that has been melted and mixed over top. Put fish with lemon butter back in refrigerator for 15 minutes before serving. When ready to serve cook at 500 degrees until done.

I use an iron skillet, because it can go from stove, ref. to oven.

Sauteid Fish

Orange Ruffie Fish or firm white fish
Flour
Egg
Clarified butter

Dip fish in flour then dip in egg and sauté in a very hot pan with clarified butter. When browned, place in 475 degrees oven until done. (about 6 to 10 minutes). Remove fish from pan and place in plate. Add a little raw butter and lemon on fish. Garnish with almonds, grapes, mushrooms chives, shrimp, and a slice of lemon.

Shrimp Soup

This is a Greek soup that I have been working on for several years. I know you will enjoy.

3 cups imported canned Italian plum tomatoes (2 cans 28oz each
1 pound shrimp (about 25)
¼ cup olive oil
1 teaspoon finely chopped garlic
1 teaspoon crushed dried oregano
4 cup fresh fish broth or clam juice
2 tablespoons drained capers
1 teaspoon dried red pepper flakes
A little Lawry's and Ms. Dash
2 tablespoon butter
¼ lb. feta cheese
4 tablespoon Ouzo, a Greek anise flavor liqueur

Preheat oven 350 degrees.

Peel and devein shrimp and set aside.

Put tomatoes in a large sauce pan and cook until reduced to 2 cups. Stir often.

Heat olive oil in another sauce pan and add garlic, stirring (do not let garlic burn).

Add a little of your cooked tomatoes to the olive oil mixture, then pour all back into the tomato pan.

Add oregano, clam juice, capers, pepper flakes and Lawry's and Ms. Dash.

Heat the 3 tablespoon butter in a heavy pan and add shrimp. Cook briefly less than 1 minute, stirring and turning shrimp until pink.

Spoon equal portions of half the sauce in 4 individual bowls, arrange 6 shrimp, plus equal amounts of the butter in which they cooked in each bowl. Spoon remaining sauce over the shrimp.

Crumble the feta cheese and scatter it all over. Place the bowls in the oven and bake 15 minutes or until bubbling.

Remove the bowls from oven and sprinkle each with 1 tablespoon ouzo and, if desired ignite. (Warm the tablespoon of ouzo with lighter and light the ouzo as you pour in bowl. Serve with good French bread loaf.

Banana Fosters

I got this recipe when I lived in New Orleans

2 tablespoons butter
3 to 4 tablespoons brown sugar
½ teaspoon cinnamon
2 bananas sliced lengthwise
¼ cup rum
¼ cup banana liqueur
2 scoops vanilla ice cream

Melt butter over low heat in a large skillet or blazer pan. Add the sugar and cinnamon and mix well. Place bananas in the pan and sauté until they begin to turn soft. Pour in banana liqueur and half of the rum and continue to cook over low heat. Heat the remainder of the rum in a small pan until almost boiling, then quickly pour it into the skillet and ignite using a long-handled spoon. Baste the bananas with the sauce until the flame dies. Serve 2 slices of banana to each portion and top with ice cream. Spoon remaining sauce over the ice cream

Cherries Jubilee

1-16 oz. can dark sweet cherries
1-16 oz. can light sweet cherries
¼ cup sugar
2 teaspoons cornstarch
1 tablespoon slivered orange peel
½ cup brandy or cognac
1 quart vanilla ice cream

Drain cherries, reserving syrup. Combine cherry syrup with cornstarch in chafing dish or electric skillet. Bring to boil. Cook and stir until smooth and clear. Add cherries and orange peel. Heat thoroughly. Pour all but 1 tablespoon of brandy or cognac over heated cherries. Pass spoon of brandy through flame until ignited or light with match and pour over cherries. When flame begins to burn down stir gently and ladle over serving of the ice cream.
Serves: 8

Lady Fingers

2 sticks butter
2 cup cake flour, sifted
½ cup powdered sugar
1 teaspoon vanilla
2 cups broken pecans

Cream butter and sugar until soft and fluffy. Add flour little at a time until used up. Add vanilla and pecans. Roll into small balls.

Bake on cookie sheet at 350 degrees, approx. 20 to 25 minutes. While warm roll in powdered sugar. Roll again when cool.

Hello Cocky Bars

1 stick butter
1 small can coconut
1 cup chopped nuts
1 can Eagle brand condensed milk
1 small package chocolate chips, semi sweet
1 cup Graham cracker crumbs

Put this in order:
Butter, Crumbs Chocolate nuts and coconut then condensed milk.
Melt butter in 9 x 9 pan. Add finely crushed graham cracker crumbs. Sprinkle chocolate chips over this then add nuts. Sprinkle 1 can coconut over this, then pour can of EBmilk over mixture.
Bake at 350 degrees for 30 minutes.
Cool before cutting in squares.

Classic Chess Pie

1 (15 oz) package ref. piecrust
2 cups sugar
2 tablespoon cornmeal
1 tablespoon all-purpose flour
¼ teaspoon salt
½ cup butter, melted
¼ cup milk
1 tablespoon white vinegar
½ teaspoon vanilla
4 large eggs, lightly beaten

Unfold piecrust and stack on a lightly floured surface. Roll into 1 (12-inch) circle.
Fit piecrust into 9-inch pie plate. Fold under and crimp. Line piecrust with foil, and fill crust with pie

CONTINUED

weights or dried beans.

Bake at 425 degrees for 4 to 5 minutes. Remove weights and foil. Bake 2 or 3 minutes until golden. Let cool completely.

Stir together sugar and next 7 ingredients until blended. Add eggs, stirring well. Pour into piecrust.

Bake at 350 degrees for 50 to 55 minutes, shielding edges of pie with foil after 10 minutes to prevent excessive browning.

Cool pie completely on wire rack.

Buttermilk Pie

1½ cups sugar
¼ stick butter
3 eggs
1 tablespoon buttermilk
¼ teaspoon nutmeg
¼ teaspoon cinnamon
1 teaspoon vanilla

Mix all and put in pie shell. Double makes 3.

Blueberries and Cream Cheesecake

2 cups gingersnap cookie crumbs (about 40 cookies)
⅓ cup butter, melted
2½ cups fresh blueberries, divided
1 tablespoon cornstarch
3 (8oz.) packages cream cheese, softened
1 cup sugar
5 large eggs
2 tablespoons cornstarch
¼ teaspoon salt

1½ cups sour cream
2 tablespoons sugar
½ teaspoon vanilla extract
¼ cup sugar
¼ cup water
Garnish: fresh blueberries

Combine cookie crumbs and butter. Press into bottom and 1 inch up sides of a lightly greased 9-inch springform pan. Bake at 325 degrees for 10 minutes. Cool on a wire rack.

Process 2½ cups blueberries and 1 tablespoon cornstarch in container of an electric blender until smooth. Cook blueberry puree in saucepan over medium-high heat 8 minutes or until slightly thickened, stirring constantly. Set mixture aside to cool. Reserve ½ cup puree for glaze.

Beat cream cheese at medium speed with an electric mixer until light and fluffy. Gradually add 1 cup sugar beating well. Add eggs 1 at a time, beating after each addition. Stir in 2 tablespoons cornstarch and salt.

Pour batter into prepared crust. Pour blueberry puree over cheesecake butter; gently swirl with a knife. Bake at 325 degrees for 1 hour, or until almost set in center. Remove from oven, and cool on a wire rack 20 minutes.

Combine sour cream 2 tablespoons sugar and vanilla in a small bowl; stir well. Spread sour cream mixture over cheesecake. Bake at 325 degrees for 10 more minutes. Cool completely on wire rack. Cover and chill 8 hours.

Combine reserved ½ cup blueberry puree, ¼ cup sugar and water in a small saucepan; cook over medium heat stirring constantly, 8 minutes or until thickened. Gently fold in remaining blueberries; remove from heat and cool.

Remove sides of pan before serving. Spoon blueberry glaze over cheesecake, allowing it to drip down sides. Garnish if desired.

Caramel Cake

½ cup shortening, butter
1½ cups sugar
1 teaspoon vanilla
2 eggs
2¼ cups sifted cake flour
2½ teaspoons baking powder
1 teaspoon salt
1 cup-plus 2 tablespoons milk

Stir shortening to soften. Gradually add sugar and cream thoroughly 12 to 15 minutes at medium speed. Add vanilla. Add eggs one at a time beating well after each. Sift flour with baking powder and salt. Add to creamed mixture alternately with milk, beating after each addition. Bake in 2 paper-lined 9 x 1½ round pans. 375 degrees-25 minutes.

CARMEL FILLING

3 cups sugar
1 cup pet milk
3 tablespoons white Karo syrup
1 stick butter

Put the above in a sauce pan; let it come to a boil, stirring all the time. In another sauce pan (I use an iron skillet) put ½ cup sugar and brown. After sugar is browned put a small amount of the first mixture in browned sugar, now put that back in first mixture and cook until a small amount put in a cup of cold water forms a firm ball.

   Cool to spread on cake

The Best Apple Cake

2 sticks unsalted butter
2 cups sugar
3 cups flour (all purpose)
2 cups chunky applesauce (I use Whitehouse chunky)
1 teaspoon cinnamon
1 teaspoon nutmeg (I grate fresh)
½ teaspoon mace
1¾ teaspoon baking soda
1 cup raisins
1 cup chopped pecans (I toast them)
1 teaspoon vanilla

FROSTING

2 cups light brown sugar
6 tablespoons heavy cream
½ stick butter
1 teaspoon vanilla
1 cup sifted powdered sugar

Preheat over to 350 degrees.
   Cream butter and sugar thoroughly. Fold in applesauce. Sift together flour, spices, and baking soda. Take ¼ cup of dry ingredients to dredge raisins and nuts.
   Fold flour mixture into butter-sugar mixture. Add vanilla, nuts and raisins.
   Pour in well buttered and floured 9 inch tube pan.
   Bake for about 1 hour, or when cake pulls away from sides. Cool in pan.
   For frosting, put all ingredients except powdered sugar and vanilla, in heavy bottom pan. Slowly bring to rolling boil, stirring constantly. Remove from heat and beat in powdered sugar and vanilla. Pour over top and sides of cake. The frosting is a hard setting one, so don't spread with a spatula.